Walking the Mist

Also by Donald McKinney
Celtic Angels

DONALD MCKINNEY

Walking the Mist

CELTIC SPIRITUALITY FOR
THE 21ST CENTURY

HODDER

MOBIUS

Hodder & Stoughton

Copyright © 2004 by Donald McKinney

First published in Great Britain in 2004 by Hodder and Stoughton
A division of Hodder Headline
This edition published in 2005

The right of Donald McKinney to be identified as the Author of the Work has been
asserted by him in accordance with the Copyright, Designs and Patents Act 1988

A Mobius paperback

A CIP catalogue record for this title is available from the British Library

ISBN 0 340 83356 4

Typeset in Sabon by Palimpsest Book Production Limited,
Polmont, Stirlingshire

Printed and bound by
Clays Ltd, St Ives plc

Hodder Headline's policy is to use papers that are natural, renewable and recyclable
products and made from wood grown in sustainable forests. The logging and manufacturing
processes are expected to conform to the environmental regulations of the country of origin

Hodder and Stoughton Ltd
A division of Hodder Headline
338 Euston Road
London NW1 3BH

DEDICATION

To Donald P. Busby, with love and gratitude.
Without you this book would never have been possible.

ACKNOWLEDGEMENTS

This book is the result of a long journey and it would be impossible to thank everyone who has made it possible. To all the people who have come to my talks; attended my workshops or who have joined the Celtic Circle, I owe you a huge debt. Thank you for your interest and enthusiasm.

I would like to thank a few people by name. First of all, Ruth Urquhart, for insisting it would happen when this book was no more than a faint idea; Cassandra Eason who encouraged, prodded and gave me the confidence to actually write it; my agent, Luigi Bonomi, for helping mould the idea and seeing the concept through to completion and especially Rowena Webb and all the gang at Hodder Mobius for their trust and belief in the book.

Finally, on a personal note, I would like to thank my family for their support; the staff at Body & Soul for their encouragement and tolerance of my absences and, most of all, Donald for all the hours of 'chats' as I sorted my thoughts out; who read and corrected all the scripts and was always there for me.

To all of you, many thanks: you've helped me make a dream come true.

CONTENTS

PREFACE

It's half past one on the morning of 21 June, the summer solstice. As I look out of the cottage window facing west, past the single candle burning on my plant-crowded desk, I can see the last pale blue remnants of yesterday. Behind, through the opposite window, already the first faint whispers of tomorrow are visible along the horizon.

I'm lucky. Where we live there are no street-lights; no noise; no cars or other trappings of city life to crowd in and spoil this magical moment. Sitting here in the dark between two days, strangely out of time, I feel at peace and certain that the time to write this book has come at long last.

Later, I shall go out into the cool night air and walk across the field to the Faery Hill. This is where I have gone for years at times of special Celtic relevance: at the fire festivals, solstices and equinoxes, I stand and share with the faeries the magic of the land. Then I will walk the sacred path to the ancient temple that stands near the crown of a nearby hill. Marked out by long-gone archaeologists, it is an ancient site of magic, where Druids and then Christian monks came to worship. I will celebrate the rising of the sun over the clear blue waters of the North Sea, on what looks to be a beautifully bright and fresh Scottish morning.

This is only the latest step in a long journey that I have travelled since 1987, and indeed before. To begin with I walked a private path of awakening and discovery as I uncovered the magical world of the Celt. Slowly, perhaps without being aware of it, I began to cast off my atheism and Western European scepticism and started to open my heart and soul to the spirits that are all around us. I started to attend the ancient village church and found peace and comfort in the simple services and its venerable tranquillity.

This book is the result of my journey. It lays out in simple steps the discoveries I have made, the truths I have learned and the sheer magic and awe that have transformed and enriched my life. This journey has been accompanied by teachings from academics, religious teachers, and friends – both human and non-human.

Slowly, I was shown that my discoveries should be shared with others. I had been helped, and now it was time for me to help, to spread the word. I started giving talks, then running small workshops all over Scotland and found hundreds of people anxious to share their experiences, though I often think I learned more from them than they did from me!

The title of the book came to me one moonless night as I was wandering along an ancient track near where I live. A heavy mist rolled slowly off the sea and over the fields towards me. Like a carpet unrolling, it was strangely unnerving although I knew I was in no danger: the track was well established. One moment the night was bright with faint stars and the Lammermuir Hills visible off to my right and then the next moment it was all gone. It was as if I could hear faint voices through the mist. Shadows seemed to slide past me, just out of sight. I strained to hear but could hear nothing, I strained to see but could see nothing. Of course, my other senses, taste, smell and touch were of little use. I floated in nothingness . . . and then I felt another sense unfurl. Slowly I became aware that I could 'sense' the wall to my side; that as I moved, I was aware of the shape of the field to my left and the occasional bush to my right. I even 'felt' the telegraph poles when I came across them. It was an amazing experience.

We all have that sixth sense. At some time all of us have entered a room or walked down a road and felt uncomfortable. How many people do we know who, when looking for somewhere to live, have talked about a sense that something wasn't right with a house?

It came to me then that Celtic spirituality requires us to act as if we are indeed walking in a mist: the accepted five senses not being sufficient for us to understand the world in which we actually live. The Celts believed that what we can see and hear is but a small part of the world that surrounds us, that there is a whole spiritual realm that we cannot explore with our physical senses.

To understand Celtic spirituality we must suspend the normal way of looking at the world and 'sense' the other worlds around us. And that is not difficult, as this book will show.

My aim in this book is simple. I want to show you, through my own experiences and studies, the magic of Celtic spirituality. I want to take the basic principles that underlined the religion of our forebears and show how we can apply them today to enrich our lives and nourish our souls.

Celtic spirituality is a rather dull technical term for something fluid and alive. Anyone can stand in nature and feel the power of the land, can understand the magic of a sacred well or spring. We can all marvel at the beauty of birds in flight or a flower in bloom, and be certain of the presence of Spirit. Indeed, if you know anything of Native American spirituality, of Australian Aboriginal teachings, or those of any other 'indigenous' people, then, as you read this book, you will recognise many of the ideas you will find in it. This should not be surprising: after all, we all live in the same world and Celtic Spirituality merely reflects our own history and culture in the words we use, the images we cultivate, the ceremonies we create and the practices we undertake. If you come from a Western background you should find the work here easy to relate to and understand. If your traditions or family background are different, it will help you to understand what makes us Celts tick!

The fluidity of Celtic Spirituality makes it hard to define. I am often asked, 'What is Celtic Spirituality?' I used to give a technical answer about changing belief and social system, but I always felt I was never quite hitting the nail on the head. After a long period of contemplation, I've come up with a radically different response.

Imagine you are sitting around a wood-burning stove in an old remote cottage somewhere in the hills and the lights are dim. It's late at night and the slumbering red glow from the wood fire just reaches out to light up your friends' faces. Together, you are all content, huddled in an intimate, warm circle of light.

As the night has grown darker your conversation has inexorably turned to ghost stories and strange tales of the unknown. As each story reaches its climax, you feel goosebumps run on your arms. Somehow you become aware of the room and even the house around you. You sense, in the darkness of the different rooms, strange ebbs and flows that you don't quite understand. You are even a little nervous: soon you will have to leave the safety of the fire and go to bed.

Of course you know there's nothing to be scared of – in fact, you enjoy the childish fear of the unknown while feeling safe in the company of your friends. Your senses seem to have expanded and you are more aware than ever. And you have a strange feeling of awe as you realise that we don't know as much as we think we do. That is Celtic spirituality.

There are three periods within the history of Celtic Spirituality. The first, or Druidic period, runs up to around AD 450, when the Druids were dominant in Celtic society. They were the bringers of religion, the advisers of kings, the news tellers, the guardians of clan history, the poets, the judges and law-givers. Truly, they were all powerful. However, we know little of what they believed or the religion they taught because they wrote nothing down. What little we know has come down to us from their enemies, like Julius Caesar who, in the mid-first century BC, portrayed them as bloodthirsty savages. But then, he was about to invade the Celtic lands of Gaul, and it was in his interest to depict the Druids as barbarians in need of Roman civilisation.

The second period of Celtic Spirituality is Celtic Christianity, which emerged in Ireland around AD 450 and lasted until around 750. It seems to have been a fusion of Druidism and early Christianity, Roman and Coptic. The reason for the conversion of the powerful Druids to Christianity has fascinated historians and theologians for generations. There is no evidence of any conflict, yet within a remarkably short period Celtic society went from paganism to Christianity.

Nowhere is this seen more clearly than in the symbol of this period: the Celtic Cross. It derives from the Druidic symbol for life: $\oplus$. It stood for the four elements of life, earth, water, fire and air, surrounded by the eternal circle of life, the serpent eating its tail. The arms of the plus sign were merely extended to make it more like a conventional Christian cross, but it is curious they should choose to do this rather than replace it with the internationally used traditional cross or crucifix.

Initially Celtic Christianity seems to have added its awareness of the spirit world and the power of nature to the teaching of Jesus and the apostles. From the Coptic Church in Egypt, it borrowed the idea of finding spiritual truth by rejecting the material world, and Celtic monks spent long periods, like the desert fathers, on retreat in remote places. St Cuthbert, for example, retreated from Lindisfarne to a tiny cell on the island of Farne. St Columba retreated to a small isolated hut on Iona and St Kessog of Luss had a huge flat stone, still called St Kessog's Stone, where it was said he sat and meditated for days without food or water. These remarkable monks, men and women, dressed like Druids; carried out the same functions as the Druids had and worshipped as they had in the forest and on the hill tops.

Gradually, however, the power and influence of the Roman church spread and from AD 750 we enter the third period of Celtic Spirituality, which lasted until around AD 1250. This was a time when the traditional ways gradually gave way to the centralising, unifying desires of the Roman church.

Even today, however, some echoes of the Celtic Druidic past remain in the systems and practices of the established churches. Harvest Festival and the continued veneration of ancient holy wells and springs still occur in both rural and urban churches. For example, although water no longer flows freely into it the holy well at St Triduana's chapel in Edinburgh is still popular with people suffering from eye problems. It is thought that Triduana was born at some time in the sixth century. She was said to be incredibly beautiful and the only daughter of the King of the Lothians. She wanted to be a nun but her father refused her requests, wanting instead to marry her to one of his neighbouring kings. Eventually a deal was struck and the husband-to-be came to call on the girl. He showered her with compliments and went to try and hold her. She struggled free and ran into the garden where she hid behind a hawthorn bush. 'What do you love most about me?' she called out. The man thought for a moment and then said it was her eyes. 'Well you may have them,' she called out and, to the horror of the suitor, she plucked out her own eyes and hung them on the bush. After that the man withdrew and Triduana was allowed to enter holy orders. The link between the Saint and this well is not known but it has been named after her since records began.

Perhaps it is this mixture of pagan and Christian that makes Celtic Spirituality so interesting and accessible today. For many, the established churches have become sterile, trapped in their mausoleums of stone and religious diktat. It is easier to find spiritual truth in a sacred grove than a dusty, half empty church hall. And I am sure that the fundamentalism and dogmatism that stigmatises much of modern Christianity alienates far more than it attracts.

Celtic spirituality is not a religion: it is a set of beliefs and practices to help us become aware of the spiritual world around us and our place in it. Whether you find it suitable to work with Jesus, his apostles and the Celtic saints, or Brigid, Mannán mac Lir and the Celtic gods, it matters little. What matters is that your life is enriched, you are at peace with your inner self and that you become aware of the magic and incredible world that surrounds us.

Nowadays I would call myself a Celtic Christian. By this I mean I believe that the unvarnished teaching of Jesus, as shown in some of the Coptic Gospels, like St Thomas's, have much to teach us about compassion and love. Equally I believe that the land and the energies that exist in it can help us to become spiritually aware, discover our life purpose and understand the true nature of God.

Finally, a word of caution. The ancient Celts lived in a world of the spoken word: nothing was written down, except by their enemies. Like many others who have studied this period, I have had to use intuition to fill the gaps. Who can know the truth? But the teachings in this book feel true. They work for me. I cannot claim to hold all the truths: others working in this area will emphasise their own views and their ways are as valid as mine. No-one can claim to know all the facts, no one has the right to dismiss your own intuitive ideas.

By the time you finish this book you should have realised the magical potential of life. You will have the tools to open yourself up to the incredible power of the land and the spiritual world that surrounds us. The shallowness and superficiality of much of the modern world will have been laid bare and you will have reconnected with what really matters in your life: you, your family and friends, and your spiritual path. I am honoured to share this exciting time with you. Use this book as a guide, enjoy your journey and relish walking the mist.

Part One

THE FIRST STEPS

1

AN INTRODUCTION

The narrow path winds up through the small glen as it tries to follow the twisting burn to its source, through the silver birches shimmering in the gentle breeze, past the dreaming alders and up, eventually, to the valley of oak trees. There two burns merge and the spot is marked by a spear of young ash. Higher up, the path leaves the burn and stumbles over rough, unkempt ground until it emerges on the low, sheep-strewn slopes of the Lammermuir Hills. From here it is a steep climb over heather-clad open ground up to the gentle undulating plateau of Dunbar Common.

Warm from the climb, I throw my jacket down on the soft bed of heather and stand drinking in the cool sweet fresh air and the sheer emptiness of the place. My soul soars free and I am truly happy.

What makes you happy? I often ask that question at talks and workshops, and it is surprising how many people find its difficult to answer. Often it is met with defensive questions – 'What do you mean?' or 'Who is happy anyway?'

Consider it now: what makes you happy? When are you most contented and at one with the universe around you? Take a moment; perhaps even write down your thoughts.

When you do find an answer it is more than likely that it won't involve money. Given that we spend most of our waking hours striving to make a wage, that is perhaps surprising. Usually people suggest something simple, like my own answer. Perhaps it's seeing your child smile, or lying in the arms of your partner. Maybe it's watching the sun rise on a clear summer morning, or simply being out with friends. Whatever the answer, the lesson is clear: the best things in life are, indeed, free.

And this is the starting point for my study of Celtic Spirituality. For as I stand there on the moor, I feel something inside stir. Something that is not part of my material body. Something that is spirit. This spirit is the core of my being, the very essence, and as I feed my material body I need to feed my spirit. These two components are not separate: they are two sides of me, which need to be nurtured in order to thrive.

What have you done recently to feed your spirit? When did you last give it the time and attention it needs? That, essentially, is what this book is about. It is a manual to help you discover and free your spirit. And as you do this, so the stresses and strains of everyday life, the problems that seem insurmountable at the moment, will be put into perspective.

More than that, a new way of looking at life will be revealed to you. A world where magic and the 'other side' are as real as your tax bill or mortgage. This is a world where a hundred times a day something special will happen to you, a world where you will find peace, contentment and a purpose in life.

The story began for me in the summer of 1987. Scottish summers are not renowned for fabulous endless sunshine so I usually take plenty of books with me on holiday. That year my partner and I were staying in a wee but'n'ben on the Berwickshire coast in south-east Scotland, not far from where we now live, and for some reason, I had only brought a couple of novels. I had soon finished them, and was forced to turn to the books left there by others on the single bookshelf. I was drawn to a concise history of Scotland.

As I read it, I was shocked to discover how little I knew about Scotland's early history. One fact in particular leapt out: that before St Andrew the patron saint of Scotland had been St Kessog of Luss, a Celtic Christian monk living on Loch Lomond in the sixty century AD. That simple fact stayed with me. It seemed to demand attention, but I did nothing about it for months. Eventually one day I found myself in Edinburgh Council's Central Library.

The Scottish Room in Edinburgh Library is a fine example of early sixties office interior design: the seats are comfortable and wooden, more appropriate to a kitchen, and the floors are laid with linoleum rather than carpet. Nonetheless, it has an excellent selection of books for someone, like myself, wanting to learn more about Scottish history.

I soon noticed that almost every book I wanted was missing. They showed as being in stock but they weren't on the shelves. I looked around suspiciously at the few other people in the room but no one seemed to have them. This was frustrating as there was indeed precious little on St Kessog and I had only a few leads. But it was as if someone had been there before me and removed them or, if the book was there, had torn out the relevant pages. It was frustrating, but also a little intriguing; like the opening of a particularly ham-fisted detective film.

Perhaps, I thought, this was meant to be. If the information was too easily obtainable then I wouldn't have valued it. Perhaps. It certainly fuelled my curiosity and endowed St Kessog with a mystical quality. Over the years, I have developed something of an obsession with him. He has been the key – the talisman, the guardian – to my whole journey into Celtic spirituality.

Unable to find out more about him, I began to research the Celtic Christian Church. I discovered that it had grown out of Ireland, spread across Scotland and into England until by the mid-seventh century it covered the whole of the British Isles except Kent. While Europe fell into a Dark Age it was the Christian Church in Ireland and Scotland that kept alight the candle of learned study and Christian teachings, albeit in unique form.

At this point all my study was academic. Indeed, when I started teaching classes in Celtic Christianity at the University of Edinburgh, I used to tell my students that I was the best person to teach this topic because I was an atheist. I could explain why people believed what they believed but that didn't mean that *we* had to accept it. I didn't believe in the spirit world or any such stuff. I was clear on that.

In retrospect, I can see that I was, however, on a path. I might not have recognised or understood it, but it was there nonetheless. Looking back, I see that there was a clear progression. It would have been impossible for me to reach where I am now in one bound. There was too much non-belief in me that had to be overcome; too much scepticism and cynicism. The path I took was slow but clearly signposted.

The first signpost was St Kessog. Without him, it is unlikely that I would have taken any interest in Celtic spirituality. I began to wonder what kind of man he had been to become a monk and live such an austere and rigorous life. It seemed as if he was reaching down to me across the years and, indeed, was there beside me; tantalisingly close, yet out of reach. Slowly I came to see that I was questing for something; some sort of spiritual truth.

But why Celtic spirituality? Why not Buddhism? Or the Church of Scotland for that matter? For me the Celts had always held some appeal. At an early age I had begun to read Neil Gunn's novels, which seemed to suggest that a mystical dimension of thought and experience was there, somewhere just beyond here.

Another indication was the music of Enya. Like many people I had thrilled to the sound of 'Orinoco Flow' and it even inspired me to have a Celtic Christmas that year – my partner bought me lots of Celtic items. It is almost embarrassing now to recall how powerful Enya was for me. But I know therapists who play it while they massage a client, and others who use it in meditation and visualisation. So I am not alone. And even if my tastes have refined and extended over the years, I am happy to admit that I still play Enya.

Also I have always loved to be in the countryside. As a child I roamed far and wide over the hills that surrounded the small town where I lived, and before that I played on the beach at Thurso in Caithness, where I was born. I have always loved the sense of wide open spaces characteristic of that most northerly county. On the moors of Sutherland or in the flat bogs of the

Flow Country it is possible almost to feel the ebb and flow of spirits on the wind. Every tuft of heather or tiny hill loch seems magical and full of hidden secrets, and on the brilliant white sandy beaches who can fail to rejoice in the sacred beauty of nature?

When I was a young adult, city life was exciting, with pubs and clubs, theatre, cinema and all the other accoutrements of a Western European lifestyle close at hand. But even then, in quieter moments, I heard the call of the wild and then I longed to escape: to turn my back on the ugly orange street-lights and race again across the wide open skies of my childhood. Although there had been that moment in 1987 when I discovered St Kessog, the wisps that make up the atmosphere of Celtic spirituality had been woven around me from a much earlier age.

However it would all have remained a very private, personal experience, but in the late 1990s two things happened. One night I had a dream. Sometimes dreams are simply a by-product of your brain filing experiences away; often they are just rubbish or fantasy. But occasionally they can be influenced by outside forces. And I think we all know when we've had a dream like that. My theory is that when we are falling asleep and when we are waking, our brain is not in touch with our normal senses and the 'sensible' thought processes that control and dismiss our inconsequential thoughts. Then, we are susceptible to subtle forces.

In my dream a voice spoke to me. It gave me a date, a few weeks off, and I was shown the beginning of a path through some trees in a plantation near where we live. Even in my dream I was puzzled, because it was an area I had passed many times and I had never seen a path there. However, when I woke I knew I had to follow the instructions I had been given: the prompting was too strong to ignore.

On the day in question I set off and was stunned to discover that, sure enough, there *was* a path, not as broad as I had dreamed – indeed, it was no more than a rabbit path, but a path nonetheless. I peered nervously through the trees, trying to see where it went. This was unknown territory for me. I hesitated, unsure of what I wanted to find and if I would find anything at all.

Eventually I climbed over the fence and traced the track through a small wood. After about twenty yards, it veered to the left and led me down the steep side of a hill. The track was little more than a whisper on bare earth. About fifteen feet down the slope, crossing the path at roughly chest height, a thick branch was suspended between two trees like a gate. A barrier, I thought, until I got closer and saw that it had been sliced in two: it was more like swing doors standing ajar to let me through. As I walked through, the voice I had heard in my dream said to me, 'For you are the Pathfinder.' Later I came to understand that I could find paths or make connections between ideas that no one else seemed to see.

The track led out on to a narrow valley floor where a small still loch seemed black in the shadow of the bright winter sun. A log served as my seat at the foot of the path looking out over the water. I had found a special place. It's a site I return to when I need its calming meditative powers, a site I would never have found if I hadn't followed my dream. That day was a special day for me and culminated with my realisation that the academic Celtic studies and the practical searching for personal spiritual truths were not two different things: they were only two aspects of Celtic spirituality. As the Pathfinder, I had been shown that I could connect the history, archaeology, theology and divination of the Celts into a coherent and understandable package.

Ten months later, the second event that was to change my personal exploration of Celtic spirituality took place. It was Samhain, or Hallowe'en, and as is my custom, I was meditating at the Faery Hill. While I was there, I became aware that I had to start going out and talking to people: I had to tell them of my experiences and open them up to encounter similar events.

This book is an ongoing part of my work. It is based on my personal experiences, the academic work that is being done in this field and the many conversations I have had during my talks and workshops. I have tried to weave it all together into an enjoyable exploration of spirituality.

There are three sections. The first deals with the basic exercises needed to explore Celtic spirituality. It will show you how to organise your life and home to help you set off along the path. You will learn how to find your first sacred place, a place which will help you take the first steps in discovering how to use nature to develop spiritual awareness. I will introduce meditation techniques to help you tap into earth energies. You will also learn how to use intuition to become more aware of the world around you, and pilgrimage to help you explore that world, both material and spiritual.

The second section gives you more tools to enhance and expand the experience. I will explore ritual, whose importance lies in the way it can combine necessary steps into an easily remembered pattern. Working closely with nature means being aware of the changing seasons and lunar cycles. These will affect what you can achieve and, by celebrating their coming and going, lead you away from abstract clock time and into a more natural and spiritual earth time. Trees are great companions and you will learn how they can help you develop your own meditation and healing skills. I shall take you into the world of faeries: these spiritual beings, closest to us, can show us the world of spirit and often work alongside us as we journey along our path. When you have mastered these areas, you will be ready to explore further meditation techniques. The section ends with a description of various divination tools and shows how they are an essential part of walking the mist.

Finally, as well as working on a spiritual level, the beliefs of the Celts affected their daily life. In the third section I will seek to show how your life can be enriched by adopting Celtic values and outlooks.

There is a tradition in Scotland, clearly seen in the Protestant churches, that religion is more than something that happens in church – for example, the Church of Scotland has its Church and Nation Committee, which comments on all political matters from wars to taxation. The belief that religion is all pervasive was almost certainly accepted by the Celts. St Columba was a member of the Dalriatan royal family and during his exile in Iona thought nothing of meddling in the appointment of a new king in AD 574.

It is important that we take this on board. To follow a path of Celtic Spirituality is to do much more than hug a tree, meditate by the sea or admire the view. You have to live the life, to walk the talk. And it is not easy. The last section of this book covers five areas of life and asks questions to which you must find your own answers. As you look at these areas – work, food, relationships, health and money – I want to challenge you to change your life; to welcome Celtic spirituality into it and learn to walk the mist.

2

GETTING STARTED

Wouldn't it be wonderful if we could recapture the magical sense of nature that we all enjoyed as children? The awe, excitement and even the eerie sense of the unseen that we all knew so well when we were young are now sadly missing for most adults. The Celts, however, lived much closer to the land than we do and were able to retain their connection with the magic. This link was important to them: to deny the hidden powers and mystical energies of the land was to deny the soul of the Celtic nation.

In Celtic lands there were no towns or cities: families lived in large farm-like units that were mostly self-sufficient. There was no money, and tradesmen plied their crafts for board, lodging and security. To the Celt, honour and courage mattered more than wealth and property. This was what we now call the Heroic Age when men and women aspired to be heroes and what your family and neighbours thought of you was more important than how wealthy you were.

For the Celt there was no division between the material and spiritual world. Magic was part of their daily life. Celtic legends and sagas are full of people who could walk between worlds, of the Tuatha dé Danaan, or Faery Folk, and heroes who were challenged or wooed by gods and goddesses and other mystical, magical beings.

Today, in our world of electricity, motorways and global television, this may seem fanciful, but Malidoma Somé tells an interesting tale. He is from the Dagara tribe in west central Africa and was born in the late 1950s. When he was just four, Jesuit priests came and selected him for special training at a Catholic seminary. Fifteen years later he escaped and eventually found his way back to his village. There he was seen as a stranger, contaminated by Western ways, and he had to learn again the customs of his people and earn their trust. In 1999 he was finally initiated as an elder of the tribe.

One day, not long after his return, he was standing with a group of tribal women. While they were talking, every now and then one would twitch or kick out at apparently nothing. Eventually he asked what was happening. They were amazed that he couldn't see the tree sprites running through the village. Their presence was so common that no one thought to comment on it.

Just because we can't see something, and it doesn't make sense to our twenty-first-century minds, that doesn't mean it doesn't exist. Like Malidoma, we are seeking to rediscover a way of life and, like the Dagara, the world of the Celts can only be truly understood if we can recognise its spiritual as well as physical aspects. Not only does that apply to everything around us, it also applies to ourselves. As we learn more about Celtic Spirituality, we will learn more about who we are and our needs in this lifetime.

In this chapter you will learn how to start meeting the needs of your spiritual self. It is the first step to becoming aware of your spiritual identity.

FIRST STEPS

Celtic Spirituality is to be enjoyed and revelled in, not suffered or struggled with, and that means you will allow to happen only what you feel able to cope with. Working with the spiritual world is a new experience and you must proceed cautiously until you become comfortable with what is happening around you. At this stage, a few simple steps are sufficient to keep you in control.

The first is to establish your home territory. To do this, you need to mark, on the ground, the boundaries of your house. This creates a safe space. It is an empowering ceremony so that you will feel secure your home. Such ceremonies were common in

Celtic times, and even today towns and villages in the Scottish Borders have Common Ridings where the folk of the town ride out along the parish borders marking the territory and sealing the land.

Marking Out Your Home Territory

First, bake some fennel biscuits. I find the following simple recipe makes lovely biscuits. Use good-quality local produce and while you mix the ingredients, think positive thoughts, or sing to the mixture. You want to have happy biscuits! Fennel is used because it is a cleanser, suppressor and protector.

A simple recipe for Fennel Biscuits.

Vary all the ingredients to taste. Take 3oz (90g) each of wholewheat flour and rolled oats. Add 1tsp of baking powder, 2oz (60g) of dark brown sugar, 2 tsp of crushed fennel seeds. Mix together. Cut 3oz (90g) of margarine into small pieces and add to the mixture. Rub together with your hands until the mixture resembles coarse breadcrumbs. Carefully add water, little by little, until the mixture forms a firm dough. Roll out on a floured board until about 1/2 cm thick. Cut into biscuit shapes and place on an oiled baking sheet in a moderate oven (350 degrees F / 180 degrees C / gas mark 4) for 15–20 minutes. Remove biscuits from oven and scatter granulated sugar over them. Allow to cool on a rack before serving.

Break up some of the biscuits and leave a trail of crumbs around the border of your garden. Ideally, do this at dusk, or during a bonfire at one of the fire festivals. As you scatter the crumbs repeat, 'Spirits of the House, protect me and all I hold dear. Accept this gift and protect me and all I hold dear.' If you prefer, you can call on another god or goddess who is important to you, or perhaps a Christian saint.

If you live in a flat, either mark the whole area of the flats or

scatter some crumbs along the outside of your windows and doors.
Choose which you feel is most appropriate for you.

You should repeat this ceremony as often as you feel necessary
and certainly every Beltaine, 1 May, and Samhain, 31 October.

Next you need a sign that you use when you start and finish
spiritual work. The Celts lived in a spiritual world and there is
no evidence that they needed this, but we do. We live in a highly
complex and multi-faceted world. Ideally our spiritual and our
'real' existence would be one and the same, but this is not so:
we cannot be contemplative and inward-looking while we are
driving the car or operating computers at work. So, we give
ourselves a sign that we are opening up our spiritual awareness
and another sign when we close down. I bow slightly to the east
when I start, and cross my arms and bow when I finish. Find
something you are comfortable with. I like something not too
visible so that I can do it anywhere at any time. But the choice
is yours. You might light a candle, say a prayer of protection that
you could compose yourself, pick up and hold a particular crystal or a crucifix. Take a moment to think about it. Don't worry
too much about it at this stage, though, because you can change
it later.

Remember that there is nothing to fear in this work: there is
no evil lurking out there. The Celts understood that there was
no such thing as demons or malicious spirits. We all like to be
scared by stories of devils and evil monsters, but that is all they
are – stories.

Of course it is easy to say this, quite another thing to live by
the teaching. I remember one night when I was walking home in
the dark along an old track that leads in a straight line from
Traprain Law, the ancient capital of East Lothian. I had just
reached the border of the farm where I live and was still a good
quarter-mile from home when I was suddenly aware that, from
behind, I could hear horses' hooves galloping along the track
towards me. Then I heard the light sound of bells. Out here they

say that the devil rides with bells so that you can hear him coming.

Of course, I dismissed this as my over-fertile imagination. But in the pitch black it is easy to get spooked. And when that happens, you're lost as your imagination plays ever more frightening tricks on you.

Gradually my pace increased. The hooves were louder and the bells more insistent. I looked back but could not see anything. The lights of the cottage were now visible ahead, but they still seemed a long way off.

I increased my pace even more. Now I was almost running. It sounded as if the hooves were nearly on me. I tried to remember the teachings. I tried to think rationally. But the urge to run was too strong. I couldn't resist that primitive instinct to flee danger. Without looking back I took to my heels.

I launched myself through the normally unused front door, barely halting to open it! I was home. Safe.

Now I can look back and laugh. I firmly believe that I was the victim of my imagination. But I had obeyed my intuition. I will never know if there really was something out there that night. And, of course, now I can even convince myself that I rather enjoyed the experience. But, of course, better safe than sorry!

CREATING A SACRED SPACE IN YOUR HOME

Your home should be somewhere that you feel safe and comfortable. It is also a practical place where you can cook and eat, sleep, entertain and relax. It has to fulfil many functions. One that is often overlooked is that it should inspire. In your home you should be able to find space and time to meditate, explore pastimes, learn musical instruments, write poetry. In the modern house even finding a comfortable space to read a book can often be difficult – but you need this inspiring, nurturing place, your Sacred Space.

It doesn't have to be large – a corner of a room is sufficient. It might only be the end of the couch where you normally sit.

It doesn't have to look different from the rest of the room. It just has to be your special space and everyone else in the house needs to know and respect that, so that when you go to sit there you don't find a surly teenager or a pile of old newspapers. It is your special space. The easiest way to show that you are claiming this area is to move things around.

For the Celt there are several components to a sacred space, and the presence of nature is the most important. My first consciously constructed sacred space was in a flat in Leith where we had a turret in a corner of one room. It wasn't as grand as it sounds, but there was a step up into a small circular area with three windows facing out over the river. There, I placed lots of green plants around a comfy seat. Nature is important because it signifies the unity that exists between all living creatures on the planet. It is, if you like, Gaia.

Next you need candles – there is something special about candlelight. Although you may not be able to light them as often as you would like, bright multi-coloured candles make an attractive addition to the space. If you wish, you can see the lighting of a candle as a ceremonial act, the opening up of your Sacred Space. Even if the electric lights are on in the room, light a candle or pass your hands over it unlit and use that as your opening ceremony instead. Remember to keep some matches nearby: there's nothing more infuriating than getting nicely settled, then having to spend twenty minutes finding a light.

You also need water – perhaps even flowing water. Inexpensive indoor fountains are widely available and you will hear the lovely, gentle calming sound of running water. Alternatively you could have a postcard with a picture of water. You could combine the fire and water by floating your candles in a bowl, you could even add nature by sprinkling in some dried petals. There are endless possibilities.

Now you need some incense: select your sticks or cones with great care so that the aroma doesn't overpower you or the other people in the house. Japanese incense tends to be more delicate and is perhaps most appropriate. You don't have to light it. To complete the four elements put some sand or earth into a small bowl, then stand the incense in it.

This is not a magical ceremony where everything has to be laid out in a special way: you are simply setting up a nice comfortable space that you will want to use. With a natural backdrop and the four elements you are creating your own little world. When you enter that world and sit in your seat, you are completing the circle: you are the fifth element.

Over time you may find that you want to add inspirational objects, or reminders of a trip you made or a person you love. These items will add to the special power of the sacred space – perhaps a picture of an ancient church you visited or a sacred temple. If you have a favourite psalm, you could copy that out and frame it. I have a modern plaque that portrays St Columba, which my partner bought for me. I often sit and muse on it, looking at the designs and thinking of this remarkable man and the world in which he lived. I also have some silver birch sticks, which I gathered from a grove of trees near where I live. I used to spend a lot of time meditating there and the sticks remind me of that.

The creation of this space is important for your spirit's sake. You need a gentle, healing place to spend time in. In modern houses there is often no space for the individual. If all else fails, why not use the bathroom as your sacred space? After all, plants generally thrive there, and what could be more relaxing and contemplative than to soak in a herbal bath by candlelight with the scent of incense to carry your thoughts to inspiring places?

KEEPING A JOURNAL

A journal is a key tool for you on your spiritual journey. Its purpose is to show you how you are progressing and also for you to write down experiences that perhaps don't mean anything to you straight away but, as you increase your knowledge and confidence, will reveal their message.

This journal is not a day-by-day diary. Far from it. It is simply to record anything that you think is important to you. For example, it might be a dream, or an idle thought while you were washing the dishes or a strange encounter with another person while you were walking down the road. Anything at all. You can also draw in it, paste in stories from the newspapers or Internet, photos, dried flowers. The only qualification is that whatever you include in it must seem important to you at the time. Even if you don't know why.

At the beginning it is also an easy way to make time for the real you. Promise yourself that for at least fifteen minutes each day, maybe just before you go to bed, you will sit and read your journal, then write or insert in it things that you want to keep.

Your journal must be private: you should feel able to write in it anything you like. Others may not understand the context of your comments or be offended by what you say about them. If you live on your own, privacy should not be an issue – just don't leave it lying around for friends to find! If you have a partner, show them the book, explain what you are doing and ask them not to read it. They should respect that. You may want to show them what you write and that is fine, but normally a journal is only for you. If you have children, you will need to consider how best to keep it private: children are naturally curious so make your plans before you go any further. It may be that you will need to keep it under lock and key, which may seem excessive – but what value your own peace of mind?

So, open your journal. If you don't have one yet get some blank paper – you can always paste it into your book later. A blank sheet of paper is always daunting. So, to help you get started, write your name at the top of the first page, then the date in the top right-hand corner. You should always start every entry on a fresh page because you might want to come back and comment later on what you wrote. Under your name, write a short para-graph describing yourself today. Don't read the next paragraph here until you have done that.

How did you describe yourself? Did you talk about your age, your job, your family, the shape of your ears? Or did you talk about your dreams, your secret self-image, your ambitions? Almost everyone always does the first, not the second. And that's fine, because that is a very important aspect of who you are. But you cannot ignore the second part either. Think about this:

Murdoch McMann

I am thirty-five. I work for a large insurance company where I am a section head. I am married, have been for twelve years, and have two children: Siobhan is seven and Lachlan is five. I live in Kirkcaldy in Fife, though I was born in Leith.

Interesting, but this tells us little about the real Murdoch. We know nothing of his likes and dislikes, his hopes and dreams, his passions and fears. We don't know if he likes himself, thinks he is too fat, too thin, boring, gregarious. We don't even know if he has any hobbies. We have no idea, if we were to meet him at a party, whether or not we would like him.

Return to your journal and complete your description. Remember, this is only for you. You need to be as honest as possible but be careful: sometimes, writing things down can make them more real than they necessarily are for you. For example, 'I hate my husband' is unlikely to be strictly true (and if it is why are you still married to him?). More likely you find him annoying at the moment, and that's fine. Admit that willingly – after all, few people are as perfect as you are!

If you find it difficult to write down an inner description, consider the following:

- What makes me feel happy?
- What makes me sad?
- Five words that describe me
- If I could change one thing about me, what would I change?

- Where do I want to be in five years' and what do I want to be doing?

The purpose of all of this is simply to give you a starting point: it's a measuring stick that will allow you to come back and see how you have progressed. You hope to build on the good things and erase the bad. But more than this, you need to recognise that there is a lot more to you, and everyone else, than meets the eye.

A big part of your journal is for recording what happens when you meditate. We will look at this in the next chapter, but in the meantime try this simple exercise.

Sitting Simply

Find a space where you feel comfortable and will not be disturbed. Make sure there is no outside noise that might irritate you. Unplug the phone and switch off all mobiles. If possible, do this in your sacred space or outside where there are lots of plants or trees. Make your sign to start spiritual work.

Close your eyes and focus on your breathing. Be very conscious of breathing in slowly, then breathing out slowly. In slowly and out slowly. Be very aware of this gentle, reassuring rhythm. Gradually you will feel your breathing slow down.

Now feel the stiffness in your shoulders and at the back of your neck. Relax your shoulders. Feel them drop down. Feel them relax.

Listen to your breathing. In slowly and out slowly. In slowly and out slowly. Be aware of your body and sense your toes, your fingers, your knees and your elbows. Relax. Sit like this for a few minutes, peaceful and self-contained.

Now get ready to start a countdown in your head. When you reach 'one' your mind will be empty of all thoughts. Slowly, with each breath in, count down: five, four, three, two, one. Now feel your mind float free. In your mind's eye see nothing, simply drift. When thoughts come into your head, listen to them, then push them away; gentle clouds in an almost clear blue sky. Seek the pleasure of drifting in emptiness.

Eventually you will feel ready to finish. Count down from five, then open your eyes. Take a moment to come round. You feel refreshed and calm. Make your sign for closure.

Write in your journal the thoughts that passed through your head. Ignore things like, 'Must remember to get the washing in', or 'What shall I make for tea?' Put down only the ones you will want to read again. You can comment on them if you want; you may want to explain to the future you why these thoughts were in your head. You might have been thinking of something you saw on television or read in a book, or of a friend and something they said or a place they had been. Whatever! The real interest is in ideas that seem to have come from nowhere. Make sure you write them down and think about them later.

This exercise is really only a form of daydreaming but it introduces one or two ideas that we will use again. In particular it is a useful tool for relaxing and it need take only a couple of minutes. Ideal for stressful family situations or at work.

MAKING YOUR FIRST ALTAR

Your sacred space is simply a space in your home where you feel comfortable. It is a little world that you complete when you are in it. An altar is quite different. Here you will create a focal point that contains items important and special to you. You will want to see and acknowledge it many times a day. It can inspire, reassure and comfort you all at once.

People have created altars since the earliest days. Many of the world religions encourage altars in the house. You will already have areas that are almost like altars. As well as overtly religious ones, we create altars when we place photos of loved ones on the mantelpiece or when we display treasured gifts where we can see them easily. Even when we pile books on a shelf or place a vase of flowers on a table we are creating a special focal point.

You can change an altar regularly. Indeed, it is important that you renew it often or it will become stale and will not attract you. We all know that at first when we have a new ornament, we spot it every time we go into the room. Then it might be months before we 'see' it again. Changing and moving things keeps them fresh and noticed.

I have a small altar in the kitchen, where we eat, cook and sit around the fire – we spend most of our time in there. The altar hangs on the wall and is a small piece of oak with a mirror behind it. All in all, it is maybe thirty centimetres long and fifteen broad. Usually I have a postcard or photo on it, a small scented candle and some stones I have gathered on recent walks. Every day I stop and look at it for a moment; I often add things or take them away. It's a simple action but it enriches my day and ensures that spiritual ideas and thoughts are kept uppermost in my mind.

So, let's devise an altar for you. Sit in your sacred space and look around you. Acknowledge in your mind all the mini-altars that you have already created. Now choose one of these sites. Think of something you want to achieve spiritually in the next two weeks. It might be to have a Celtic evening, a time of tranquillity, with a scented bath, inspiring Celtic music[1] and meditation. Place on your altar something to mark each of these experiences – a candle or two, some flowers and a picture in a frame of a musician who inspires you. Or perhaps you want to go for a walk in the woods; gather some pine cones and put them into a bowl. It doesn't have to be ostentatious, just meaningful for you.

As you proceed through this book think about what you are learning and doing and let it influence how you tend your altar. You will want to introduce signs of the changing seasons, symbols of major events that are happening to you and the world around

---

[1] See Further Listening List.

you, to celebrate the great Celtic festivals and much more. You might want to add postcards from friends on holiday, berries from bushes in the garden, a photo of a loved family member. The list is endless.

If you already follow an established religion, be sure not to exclude it from your altar; seek out small statues or photos to use. If you are a Christian why not include a cross made of ash wood? The Celts believed that ash is the great tree that connects the inner and outer; heaven and earth, so this particular wood is ideal.

Your altar should be tended with love and care. Take time over it and enjoy it. The attention you give it reflects your own spiritual awareness and development. A neglected altar says too much about you and your lifestyle.

You can have as many altars as you want – one in every room if you so desire. It's up to you. If you have a garden then an altar there is also a great idea. Choose trees and plants carefully and create a small secluded spot for yourself. To be able to sit in a sacred space outside with an inspiring altar surrounded by aromatic plants and sheltered by trees is truly one of the great Celtic experiences.

SPIRITUAL INFLUENCES

So far, we have concentrated on creating the right environment to help you become more aware of spiritual influences in your life. You will notice them more and more. Now I want to introduce you to three of my favourite ways of acknowledging and welcoming the spiritual world.

Using an inspirational card gives each day a positive start. The most famous of these are the Findhorn Foundation's little *Angel Cards*, each of which features one uplifting and empowering word, like *'joy', 'peace', 'fulfilment', 'harmony'*. Put them in a small bowl and have them handy, perhaps in the hallway or on the dining-table. Each morning pick one out and think about the word during the day.

You can see it as a message from your guardian angel. After all, how do you choose one card over another? They all look the same but somehow you do select one: perhaps something, or someone, is helping you. Of course, they are all uplifting and inspiring but the one you pick is almost always strangely relevant to the moment. Keep a set at work and share them with workmates or friends: people love to choose a card, which may spark interesting and rewarding conversations.

You could start writing poetry. I don't do enough of this. The ancient Irish for poet was *file* (fem. *velitas*), literally 'seer'. Poets were highly regarded in Celtic society and often composed in secret. There are many tales of them sitting in dark caves conjuring words up from other worlds. Because of this, the poets were thought to be able to access spiritual powers and the poems themselves to have magical properties.

There is indeed something mysterious and otherworldly about composing poetry. When you've completed a poem, you will feel a great sense of achievement. We have all gone through phases, often when we were teenagers, of writing *Angst*-ridden verse, but it can be uplifting and joyful too. Make a special event of writing a poem. Choose a time when you can have the house to yourself. Use your sacred space and altar to inspire the bard in you and record the result in your journal. Or go out to walk in the countryside or by the sea and seek inspiration from nature. You'll be amazed by how talented you actually are!

My favourite exercise is so simple. The Celts were entranced by the idea of dusk. They believed that this was when the veil between the worlds was at its thinnest. It is also the time when nothing is quite as it seems. Dusk is almost impossible to capture, the elusive point when daylight gives way to darkness.

When you set off on a walk at dusk it is still essentially light, but getting darker. When you look about, you can still see everything as it appears in daytime. Gradually that changes; bushes that are familiar during the day take on odd new shapes in the dusk and everything becomes a little strange. We have a scrawny misshapen gorse that we call the Buddha bush because at dusk it takes on the exact outline of the Chinese Buddha in repose.

Truly, dusk is a most inspirational time because you can let your imagination run wild. You may see old crones hiding in the bark of ancient oaks, faeries and light-beings dancing in the lanes, odd shapes gliding through the trees and, if you're lucky, the moon rising over nearby hills.

If you live in a city or town, you can still share some of this magic. If you have a garden, create in it a sacred space and watch the world change around you as darkness falls. If you live in a flat, find some parkland where it is safe for you to be after dark. If that is not possible find a view from one of your windows that will allow you to enjoy the lengthening shadows and the magic of this time of the day.

It is at this time that the spirits may whisper to you and influence your ideas and fancies. When you imagine a doorway in the hillside, how do you know that there isn't one? When you feel an angel's wing brush your face, how do you know that it hasn't? And when familiar places seem to have transformed into magical groves, could it not be that we are only now seeing the magic that is always there?

3

YOUR FIRST MEDITATION

Now I am going to introduce you to a particular technique for meditating. The beauty of it is that you can use it anywhere and at any time. I have meditated on the top of hills, in my lounge, lying in the bath, even on a sunbed.

There is no evidence that the ordinary Celt meditated, but as they were much closer to the land than we are, they probably retuned their minds more instinctively than we can. Celtic monks and Druids certainly meditated. Monks spent days in retreat. Many famous ones, like St Kentigern and St David, craved peace and quiet for contemplation and in this they were probably replicating the actions of the Druids.

WHY MEDITATE?

Meditation can be defined as a method of emptying your mind of all the unimportant clutter that distracts you from the more important matters of life.

There are many reasons why people meditate. For some it is a way of relaxing, of switching off from the pressures of daily life: there is nothing mystical or spiritual about it and, in fact, it is more or less the same as the Sitting Simply exercise on page 20. Meditation shows up the unimportance of the huge amount of repetitive and routine thoughts that preoccupy us and so helps us keep things in perspective. How often have you spent a sleepless night worrying over something that even by the morning has become less important? Or wasted several hours on the Internet trying to find out about something that you'll forget about almost immediately? Try to apply the two lessons that the following exercise seeks to teach.

Learning Not to Worry

Take a sheet of paper and make a list of everything you've worried about or been preoccupied by today. You might include something that happened at work, what your children were up to, ideas on how to spend your summer holiday, or whether to buy a new three-piece suite. If you can't think of anything, carry a small notepad around with you during the day and jot down any major worries as they occur to you.

Now put the list away. Hide it is a place where no one will find it – perhaps seal it in an envelope addressed to yourself and stash it below your jumpers in a cupboard. Mark a date a fortnight away on your calendar and on that day retrieve the envelope. Before you open it, write down as many of the things you were worried about as you can remember. More than likely you'll have forgotten most of them. When you look at the list you wrote, you'll see how petty or short-term most of the worries and preoccupations were. Some might still be current but almost all of them will have been resolved.

Now leave the list for a month. That's six weeks in total. Then three months. Then a year. After five years you'll even have forgotten what your notes meant.

Of course, you know even now what the result of the exercise will be but continue with it. My experience is that it's only by doing it yourself that the truth comes home to you that we spend a huge amount of time and energy worrying about trivia or things we can do almost nothing to resolve.

When I did this, I was shocked by how short term and utterly irrelevant to my life most of my concerns were. Work dominated, of course, with real anxiety attacks over what, with the benefit of hindsight, turned out to be nothing. And as I realised that, I began to resent it. And as resentment grew, so did my determination to do something about it. So, this exercise should motivate you to start looking seriously at the issue.

One of my aunts always says of her husband, 'Solve his problem, and he's another three waiting for you.' By nature humans are worriers – maybe it's one of our defining characteristics – but we need to curb the tendency, control it and keep it firmly in its place. Meditation helps us do that.

But meditation is far more than this. For many it is a central part of their religious experience. It is the means they use to transport themselves from the awareness of one world, this material plane, to the spiritual dimension or areas, at least, of non-material awareness. Buddhists aim to move themselves into pure awareness, a state of complete openness and balance with the true nature of reality. One famous book has the dramatic title *If You Meet Buddha On the Road, Kill Him*: it means that if you come across an image of the Buddha while you are meditating, you are being distracted and must rid yourself of it.

Many modern Christian groups use meditation techniques as well. Some see it as a tool to empty your mind the better to hear the Word of God. Others use Christian imagery – for example, they picture Jesus Christ as a guide to lead them through visualisations. Angel meditations are very popular with Christians and non-Christians alike. This is where angels can work with us to help us in our lives, or act as inspiration to help us attain a higher spiritual awareness.

For pagans, depending on their tradition, meditation is usually a precursor to shamanic journeying, in which a leader will accompany them into the spiritual realms in the belief that whatever ails them in this world can be healed by actions taken in the Otherworld. Today many people view the Druids as early shamans. Although there is no real evidence for this, their reported use of drugs and trances suggests that it is possible.

Whatever the background, there are good medical reasons to meditate. Studies have shown that people who meditate regularly are calmer, less likely to suffer from stress-related diseases and more contented with their lives. Generally they live longer and visit the doctor less frequently than those who do not meditate.

BEING AWARE OF TIME

Meditation is not complicated but neither is it easy. It can be difficult to maintain it. Once you reach a stage where your mind is clear and open, time should mean nothing and minutes should turn into tens of minute without you noticing. That is hard to achieve: time, it seems, demands our attention.

Let's tackle the issue of time first. Today everyone's attention span seems to be getting shorter. To be able to spend sizeable periods of time contemplating ideas and working slowly through problems you will need to overcome this. Gradually you will master the art of emptying your mind and only slowly will you come to understand what different imagery and ideas mean to you. This is a lifetime's work, or even several lifetimes'! But then you would not believe it possible to learn to drive in one lesson, or be competent at *t'ai chi* after thirty minutes' tuition: It is the same with meditation. You cannot appreciate all the spiritual implications of a classical Irish poem on one hearing or grasp the emotional stimulation experienced by the artist of a landscape painting after one short viewing. To acquire deep understanding, you need to study, to contemplate, to take time and be patient.

Being Patient
Visit the seaside. While you are there check to see if the tide is coming in or going out and try to judge whether it is moving quickly or slowly. If it is coming in, measure a distance that you think the tide will reach in ten minutes or so and draw a line in the sand, or choose a particular stone or other marker. Take off your watch if you wear one. Stand and vow not to move until the tide has reached the marker. If the tide is going out place a stick in the sand and vow not to move until the base of the stick

is permanently clear of the water or choose a submerged stone and vow to remain until the stone is uncovered. As you stand there, listening to the sounds of the waves, be aware of their constant never-ending energy. Try to feel the ebb and flow as each wave washes in and sweeps out. The Celtic monks performed a version of this exercise: they would stand in the water knee deep, sing psalms and pray aloud until the water reached their neck. Not only would that have taken great patience and tolerance, it would, in this climate, have been distinctly uncomfortable.

The trick here is not to be too ambitious. Often the tide moves slowly and you might be trapped for hours. When you have done this exercise once, don't try it again that day (unless you only waited a couple of minutes) as you will quickly lose tolerance and give up too easily.

A different option is to wait for a sunny day, then mark off changes in a particular shadow. As the sun moves across the sky, watch how the shadow moves on the ground, then make a mark a short distance ahead. Stand and watch the shadow until it strikes your marker. The advantage of this method is that you can come back day after day and measure your progress: although the sun changes position, it is a far more gradual process than it is with the tides.

On use the light of the full moon, on a clear night track the moon through the branches of a tree or the shadow it casts of yourself. My own favourite is to watch the moon rise from behind a nearby hill with the trees silhouetted black as it slowly climbs clear of them into the night sky. We have left behind in our sterile, polystyrene world the ability to tune into the natural rhythms of the earth. This exercise will enable you to access it.

Learning to slow down and be aware of the pace of nature is difficult but necessary for our spiritual work. Watching how different plants and trees move from winter to spring to summer is a humbling and rewarding experience. There can be real exhilaration and joy in noticing the first tentative opening of buds on a plane tree or spotting the first snowdrop after a long bleak winter.

BREATHING

Here is another simple exercise, common to many forms of meditation, which involves the most basic human act. This, unlike Being Patient (see page 29), seeks to change your awareness while you are sitting.

Breathing Meditation
Find a quiet place where you will not be disturbed. Your sacred space would be ideal or a place in your garden. Make yourself comfortable and relax slowly. Close your eyes. Be well within yourself. Feel comfortable sitting; feel safe and content.

Now become aware of your breathing. As you do this you may feel a slight sense of alarm and an increase in your breathing rate. This is perfectly normal and shouldn't cause you any unease. It's almost as if your body is suddenly self-conscious because you are paying attention to something that normally you hardly notice.

Within a couple of seconds your breathing should settle down again. Wait for a short time and now slow your breathing fractionally. How does that feel? If it is uncomfortable, return to your normal breathing pattern, sit for a few more minutes, then try again. As we relax and de-stress, our breathing should slow naturally.

Now, with your breathing that little bit calmer and slower, feel your whole body relax and soften with each breath out. Feel your shoulders slump and your back become less rigid. Concentrate on each intake of cool breath. Take a slow, long, deep inhalation: feel the air come into your body and refresh you. Now exhale. Take another deep breath and again imagine the clear, fresh air of the hilltops in spring. Feel it come into your body and cleanse you. Now exhale.

Concentrate on this for a couple of minutes and then, when you are ready, pay attention to how you are breathing out. Breathe out slowly through your mouth and feel the air hot and heavy with moisture slipping from you. Now inhale cool fresh air. And exhale the air, hot and moist.

Focus on this for a while and you will become aware of what else is happening, even without thinking about it. As you breathe in, the air fills your lungs and your abdomen expands to cope with the increased volume. As you exhale, your abdomen contracts and pumps the air out of your lungs, up and through your mouth. Your body is an incredible machine.

Think about this operation as you breathe slowly in and out. Feel the circle of actions within your body. There is something comforting about its regular, cleansing nature. It lets you know you are alive.

Sit like this for maybe five minutes or until you find your mind wandering. Then, slowly, become aware again of where you are sitting and what surrounds you. After a few seconds, open your eyes.

The simplicity of this exercise is deceiving. It is used in various forms by religious groups around the world to teach people not only to sit quietly and still the mind but also to remind them of the incredible nature of the machine that is the human body.

THE MEDITATION TECHNIQUE

When I started exploring meditation, my main aim was to find a method that was simple and, more importantly, worked. At workshops I attended I always seemed to struggle with the techniques: they never seemed real enough to me. Of course, eventually I was led to one that worked well. Over the years I have adapted it but you can find it in its original form in *Handbook for Light Workers* by David Cousins.

The Meditation Exercise

Before you start this exercise, be aware of where you are and the nature of the ground on which you are standing or sitting. If you are inside, perhaps in your sacred space, you need to take a moment to check the nature of the soil around your building. The reason for this will become evident shortly.

Make your sign to start spiritual work. Now plant both feet firmly on the floor or ground. You can do this in either a sitting or standing position, it doesn't matter. If you are outside and you feel comfortable doing it, remove your footwear so that your bare feet are in contact with the earth. This doesn't affect the meditation as far as I'm aware but it just feels good.

Close your eyes. Imagine roots, like plant roots, coming out of the soles of your feet and growing down into the soil. Watch it in your mind's eye. You know what the soil is like where you are so it is easy to see and feel this happening.

When you are ready, feel the earth energy being sucked up by the roots, like water, and rising through your body. You might find this easier to achieve if you think of your breathing as a pump: with each breath in, you pull more of the energy through your body. Feel it enter your feet slowly, then rise up your legs, through your torso, up to your shoulders and down your arms, up your neck and eventually to the crown of your head. Feel your body filled with the glowing energy. In your mind's eye see it like a glass vessel full of deep red clay or golden sandy loam or whatever kind of soil you have. See it not only from the outside but from the inside as well.

Hold that sensation for a moment, then pull a beam of pure white light down into the crown of your head and feel it wash away all the soil filling your body and replacing it with healing white energy instead. Feel it wash through your head, neck, arms and torso, down your legs and into the roots. Feel the energy feed the earth beneath you. Feel your body glowing with white light.

Now repeat the exercise. Pull the earth energy up through your body with each breath, bringing the earth through you until, once again, you are a being of the soil. Now hold that sensation. Feel the power of the earth. Be a being of the earth. Call down the white light and wash your body clear of the earth. Feel the pure love of white light radiate from you into the soil. Hold that feeling.

For a third time call up that elemental earth energy. With each breath, feel the power rolling through you slowly, steadily and inexorably. Feel the soil as it fills you with its reliable strength. Feel as the earth feels, be as the earth is, rejoice as the earth rejoices. Now call down the white light and wash away the soil. Feel the light and energy of the white light course through you, liberating you from the earth and reconnecting you to the light. Now you are a light-being again, complete and pure. Feel the exhilaration of that purity and know that you are invincible.

Now, still holding that white light within you, feel your mind empty. If it helps concentrate on your slow breathing. When you are ready, float, safe and serene. If any images or ideas come into your head acknowledge them and let them drift away. Be happy and content.

To begin with, you may feel that you can only hold that sensation for a couple of minutes, but as you practise this meditation, you will find that you can do this for longer and longer. Be there for as long as it feels comfortable.

When you are ready to end, begin to close down. Imagine your roots slowly retracting from the ground. Now become aware again of where you are and what is going on around you. Wait for a few seconds, then open your eyes. Make your sign for the closure of spiritual work.

This is a powerful meditation and you will probably feel a little disoriented when you finish. This is nothing to worry about. Sit or stand quietly for a few minutes until you feel ready to move on. Write in your journal any images or significant thoughts you experienced. Don't think about them too much now – that may be hard because they may be vivid, but it is best to wait, maybe for a couple of days, before you try to understand what, if anything, they mean.

Do not underestimate the intensity of this exercise. The simple repetition three times of pulling the earth energy up and the light energy down takes your awareness away from the material world and places it in a different plane. If you stop at that point you will still feel disoriented. It is necessary to repeat the exercise, and while it may seem time-consuming to begin with, you will quickly become familiar with it and be able to do it in a few seconds if necessary, though I like to take my time to thoroughly enjoy and explore the different sensations.

This exercise is at the very centre of the spiritual practice I am laying out in this book. It is worthwhile therefore to work with it until you are happy with it. You should aim to do this exercise every day if possible either in your sacred space or at your altar. The easiest way to achieve this is to fit it into your daily schedule. For example, do it as soon as you get up, or before breakfast, or just before you go to bed. There is no set time, just whatever fits in with you. If you can't do it every day, don't worry: just try to meditate as often as you can.

Don't be disappointed if nothing seems to be happening. You hear stories of golden angels, or Earth Goddesses or Faery Queens appearing, but that is not what we are trying to achieve here. All we are trying to do is to start a process of retuning your mind to make it more open and sensitive to spiritual influences. Regular meditation gives the part of your mind that is open to these matters the space to expand – to reach out. To begin with, the process will be hesitant and uncertain, and any experiences you come across in the early days are best written in your journal and forgotten about. Come back to it in a year and you'll laugh at some of the things that you thought were so profound. If anything is significant, it will recur or, at least, be written down for you to dwell on.

In the beginning one of the images I kept seeing was clouds. It seemed to me that I was sailing over a cloud-hidden landscape with just the occasional exasperating snapshot of land. I was sure that if I could only recognise it, it would be significant. Eventually I realised, after much time and effort, that I was reliving images I had seen from a plane. Now when that happens when I meditate, I just laugh and push it aside. In the early years, though, there were pages and pages of pointless speculation and postulation in my journal.

This meditation technique connects us with the two other realms, like the giant ash tree with its roots in the earth and its top branches reaching to the heavens. The white light connects us with a higher plane, the spiritual, or angelic, plane; the light is pure, cleansing, loving energy and it is always available to us. Sometimes I imagine a great shower of white light and I step into it and let it wash away all the debris of everyday life. I step out the shower reinvigorated and energised.

The roots into the earth are a powerful symbol for the connection we need to make between ourselves as biological machines and the world of nature that surrounds and nurtures us. Whether you are sitting in your garden, lying in the sun or simply touching a tree, meditation will heighten the experience and make it even more rewarding. In the next chapter we will explore this idea further by using the technique at a site of ancient wisdom you will find for yourself: your first sacred site.

4

FINDING YOUR FIRST SACRED SITE

The Celts had a strong sense of place. It was of crucial importance to them is deciding where to build their houses, castles and
forts, where to worship and even how to lay out their fields and
tracks. They acknowledged that there were energies in the land
that not only attracted different spirits and gods but manifested
in this world by helping or hindering man's efforts. They almost
certainly approached the Druids for advice on selecting the most
appropriate spot to build a house or to plant their crops for an
enhanced yield.

The early monks also knew this and their churches were almost
certainly built on former Druidic sites, which might well have
been venerated since man first came to these shores. It is interesting to consider how the power in the land has been tended by
different holy orders. It has certainly been my experience that
old churches built on ancient sites have more of a sense of presence than those built where it was convenient, in the middle of
a new housing scheme, for example.

Aberlady is a small coastal village in East Lothian about ten
miles east of Edinburgh. Its Angle name was Aber Lessic, literally 'at the mouth of the path'. The path referred to could well
be a ley line – a line of psychic energy that courses round the
surface of the planet. Studies have shown that all major and most
minor Neolithic sites – standing stones, stone circles, burial
mounds – all lie in straight lines, one of which runs across the
river Forth from the Lomond Hills in Fife to Traprain, an ancient
volcanic plug that dominates the East Lothian plains.

Until the Reformation Aberlady was an important ecclesi-
astical site and the small parish church is well worth a visit. The

only problem is that it is not where you might expect it to be. Because of its history, you would have expected it to stand on the ley line, but it doesn't: it lies on high ground to the west of the village. This mystery was solved for me by an old local man who revealed that the original stone church had stood in a different spot, on a spit of land that reached out into the river Forth where it was flooded regularly. It was moved to higher ground in the sixteenth century. Why build a church where the river floods? The answer, of course, is that it had to be constructed on the ley line.

In this chapter I will help you find your first sacred site. A sacred site can be anywhere. It is a place that will become very important to you. It might be somewhere dramatic, like a ring of standing stones, or, it may simply be a favourite park bench. It might be a dramatic cliff overlooking the sea, or a meadow on the side of a hill. There is no set formula for finding a site. It is personal, something just for you.

What all sacred sites contain is the ability to enhance and stimulate your meditations. They will inspire and instruct you, enthuse and confuse you. That is the joy of them. When you visit and meditate at these sites, they may enhance your innate psychic abilities through earth energies that exist there. Perhaps it is just the presence of a particular stone, crystal or even naturally occurring gas that is enough to change your perceptions. Who knows? The key at this point is not to dwell too long on why something is happening, but on the outcome. At the end of the time you spend at your sacred site, you should feel that you have enjoyed quality spiritual time and, in some small way, have increased your understanding of spiritual matters. You should see your life in a wider context as spiritual truths colour your perceptions of your daily life.

No site is better or worse than any other. Each is unique, and it means nothing that dramatic monuments have been placed at some. Standing stones, for example, were probably erected on a site that had already been declared sacred. Maybe one day someone will erect a monument on your site.

Different people are drawn to different sites, so once you have found yours, keep it special for yourself. If friends come with you and complain that they can't feel anything, that means only that the site is not for them. Of course, it is reassuring when someone else can feel the energy of a site, but you must trust your own instincts. I was told of a site in the Glasgow Botanic Gardens down near the river and I went there full of expectations because the person who had told me about it was someone I respected. It was a pretty site, but it did nothing for me.

WHERE TO GO

My first site was a place I had visited several times before with friends. I was quite shocked when I realised that it had spiritual significance for me. And this is often the way. You are on a spiritual path and you have been led, or pushed, down it. You will have been guided several times to visit your sacred site but were probably too intent on other matters to sense anything special about it. Or maybe you just didn't understand what you felt, or didn't know what to do about it.

Now you are going to try to open yourself up to the whispering of the angels. The spirits that surround us will tell us where we need to go to begin our journey.

Finding Your First Sacred Site
Make the sign for starting spiritual work and do the Meditation Exercise (see page 33).

Now you are floating in a warm, dark cloud. Feel calm and at peace. Feel happy and carefree. Be aware that an anchor holds you to your body. Feel it like a silken thread connecting you to your world.

You are still floating in your warm, dark cloud. You are still at peace and still calm. You are feeling happy and carefree. You are smiling and contented.

You want to find your sacred site. Suddenly you know that

this is what you want more than anything else. You want to find your Sacred Site. Silently, in your mind, say, 'I want to find my sacred site. I want to find my sacred site.' Chant it softly to yourself like a mantra: 'I want to find my sacred site. I want to find my sacred site.'

Now you know that this is what you want. Feel the urge to go there. Feel the strong desire building inside you. It's so strong. And growing stronger. The spirits are gathering around you. The angels want to show you your sacred site.

'I want to find my sacred site. I want to find my sacred site.'

Your desire to find it is building up inside you like water behind a dam on the point of bursting. Feel the yearning. Like a pain, like a love affair.

Hold the urge. Now, in your mind's eye, see an ancient wooden door with big black hinges and a wrought-iron handle.

Feel your desire.

Reach out and grasp the handle. When the door opens outwards, you will step through and into your sacred site.

Take a deep breath. Feel your desire.

And open the door.

Now you're there!

Now that you can see the place where you must go, you almost laugh. It seems so obvious. Pause for a few moments and look around, remembering in your mind's eye what it is like. Now you understand. Now you know. Enjoy the sense of being there and anticipate visiting it physically.

Now you are ready to return. Slowly become aware again of your body and what is going on around it. Feel yourself return; feel your fingers and toes. Wait a few seconds, then open your eyes. Make the sign for the end of spiritual work.

If nothing happens when you do this visualisation, or if you are not sure that the site was chosen for you, write down your experiences, your doubts and uncertainties, then wait a few days and try again. You could also try visiting the site, not to do anything but just to see how it feels to be there. Are you contented or apprehensive? At home or strangely ill at ease? And how about the land? Does it seem glad that you're there or do you sense hostility, apathy even? From all of this, you will know if it is the right site for you. If you have any doubt at all, it is probably not the right site for you at this point in time.

PREPARING TO GO

Until now you have been working in a safe space that you have created in your own home. Now it is time to go into 'the field'. As with all fieldwork there is a level of unpredictability about it. All we can do is try to cover every likely eventuality, then cross our fingers and hope for the best.

The first stage is to get comfortable with the sacred site. Spend some time there. Watch what happens. Are there a lot of people? If there are then you need to find a time when it's quiet. Are there animals: cattle or sheep maybe? Again you need to find a time when you will not be disturbed. You are going to visit this site and meditate at it, so you must be familiar with it and at ease while you are there. That may take some time, depending on the site and how you feel about it.

It may even take ingenuity. One woman told me that her site was a park bench in the Princes Street gardens in the middle of Edinburgh. She meditated there by buying reflective sunglasses and holding a newspaper. No one could see that her eyes were closed, and no one was likely to disturb her while she was 'reading' the newspaper.

Also, decide in advance if you need to take anything with you. For example, if you want to sit at your site, are there any chairs, or will you have to bring something with you? If it is a particularly exposed site, you might need extra clothing; if it is muddy, you will need sturdy boots.

On the day of the visit, there is a ritual to be observed that will enhance the experience: a cleansing exercise that will help you distance yourself from your day-to-day life. The Celts would have immersed themselves in the sea or river as a ritual cleansing but I find a simple shower suffices. The tradition of cleansing oneself in water before a spiritual experience continues to this day in many southern European countries: in Andalucía on the day of San Juan, 23 June, great bonfires are lit along the beaches and people submerge themselves in the sea. They even take water home to sprinkle around the house.

After the shower, dress yourself slowly in natural fibres, then tend your altar and your sacred space. While you are doing this think about the site you are going to visit and try to imagine what it will feel like to be there and to do the meditation exercise. About an hour before you set off, try to find time to do the Breathing Meditation (see page 31). It will be good practice and will heighten the experience of walking to the site. All of this is part of the ritual cleansing process.

Fast, if you can, until after your visit. Or take some food with you: bread or fresh fruit and water are best.

Do as many of these things as you can. Don't worry if you are unable to follow it all. Often I take a notion to visit my sacred site and just go. The ritual cleansing makes more of an event of it, and you should use it at least for your first visit.

Once you are ready, set out for the site. It is best to walk, if possible. As you go, think of the site and anticipate the sensations you will have when you are there. If it is close, in your garden, for example, then go for a short walk first.

As you approach the sacred site take time to view it before you move on to it. If possible walk round it, try to see it with fresh eyes, as if you have never been there before. You'll be amazed at how many new things you notice every time you visit.

MEDITATING AT YOUR SACRED SITE

Because each site is so different, I would like to describe what happened to me at my site – the old temple at the top of Doon

Hill in East Lothian, near where I live. It will let you work out what would be most suitable for you to do at yours.

The first couple of times I visited the site I went by car, but there was a walk when I arrived that took about an hour. I had done it once before. Ever since I had realised that the temple was important to me, I had felt a physical calling to it, a yearning from deep within me. I knew I had to walk and take what I now know as the sacred path: an old path that spirals clockwise up the side of the hill.

From the crown of the hill I looked down on the temple, which is a little lower and sits in a hollow. As ever, the wind was rushing around me and the few trees and bushes seemed to have their shoulders hunched against the cold early-winter gusts. Even the grass, pale green and windswept, seemed stoically resigned to the weather.

I was warm from the climb and strode down over the field to the site. The outline of the temple is marked out in concrete so it is easy to see how the building and stockades were shaped. I wandered round it and chose to enter by the gate, as presumably the Druids would have done. I approached the temple clockwise. I had a strong sense that I was trying to replicate what people long since gone had done but whose actions echoed on.

Here the wind seemed less severe and the temperature more moderate. I stood in front of where I thought the shrine would have been but that didn't feel right. I moved around a little until I found a spot that felt better. It was there that I did the meditation, standing up and facing due east.

From my journal I see that I felt as if I was falling backwards, almost as if I was levitating. I floated there until I saw, in my mind's eye, a shape in front of me. Curious, I allowed myself to focus on it and saw that it was an eye in the face of an old man wearing an animal headpiece. He looked like the archetypal shaman and seemed to be gazing down the years at me with some curiosity.

I pulled myself away from the image with some difficulty, and the next puzzled me for some time: it was a white plaster cast of two hands clasped in prayer. Now I recognise it as a symbol showing that there had been some kind of Christian site there at one time.

I was reassured by this as I felt that I had plugged into the site. Subsequent adventures and study have reinforced my view that the site had been used as, first, a Druidic site, then later as a Christian church.

Interestingly I also discovered a local legend that witches had danced on that spot long before archaeologists looked at aerial photos and saw the signs of buried buildings.

So, I had approached the site with respect and awareness. I had tried to go with the flow, to fit the history as I knew it, then used my intuition to feel my way to the perfect spot for meditating.

AFTERWARDS

It is important that immediately afterwards you write all your experiences in your journal. I find it easier to do this by moving to another place not far away: this breaks the spell of the site and lets you think coherently. You will know which of your thoughts and images were self-created and which seemed to come from a deeper or outside source. Leave analysis of what happened until later. Simply enjoy recording your feelings and experiences, then put away the journal.

Sometimes you might select a site, do all the preparations, meditate there and nothing happens. That is fine. The important question you should ask yourself afterwards is: did I feel comfortable at that site? If you did then you need to visit it a few more times while you learn to 'tune in' to the energies. If you didn't feel comfortable, or couldn't find the right spot to stand, or felt uneasy, the site is probably not for you. From time to time we all misunderstand what we are shown. For instance you might have seen some parkland and assumed your sacred site was in the nearest park – but perhaps it was another park and you jumped to the wrong conclusion.

I have misunderstood several visions. One of the sites I was guided to visit was Melrose. The abbey there is ancient and existed in St Cuthbert's time, the late seventh century, so it seemed a plausible site. The ruins of the later fifteenth-century building are high and austere but they give a good impression of what a tremendous building it must have been.

I sensed nothing. For a religious site with such a noted history, I might have expected to pick up some resonance, but no.

In old English Melrose means 'bend in the river', which puzzled me as there was no bend. Later I learned from someone at one of my talks that the original abbey lay a little to the east of the town and there the river bends right round to form almost an island on which the abbey stood.

Try to visit your sacred site often while you get to know, understand and appreciate it. Try to read up on any local history. Check old maps; local libraries often have locally produced histories of the area. You may be drawn to a drab piece of wasteground in the city and despair, because of its plainness and lack of inspiration but try to discover what stood there before. Perhaps a river flowed through it, or there was a beautiful garden for a large house now demolished or a monastery. Old people who have lived locally all their lives often have tales to tell. Don't be afraid to ask: they often enjoy reminiscing.

Study Ordnance Survey maps and look for evidence of possible ley lines. Key indicators are hilltops, unusual geographical features, castles, ancient churches and standing stones. Try to find straight lines that connect as many of them as possible with your sacred site. You can spend many happy hours discovering your area. Even if nothing relates to your site, it will help you appreciate the locality. The Celts did not live in cities so all the land now under concrete and tarmacadam has only been hidden for a comparatively short time. You need to reach under it to the heartbeat of the land, which is still there.

Your site may not be geographically significant, but other factors may have drawn you there – the trees, bushes and plants, perhaps. They all attract spirits and can generate their own strong presence. Think of the cool, calm serenity of walking through a natural, unplanned forest. Often the Celts worshipped in groves where the different trees would be included in their sacred practices.

The key point is to be relaxed about it. You have selected a site for some reason and you have to work with it to find out what it is.

You may feel you would like to bring back something from the site to your home. If you do, go to the site and ask aloud for permission. See how it feels. Pick up a stone or some sand and see whether it feels right to take it away. Never dig up a plant or cut a branch from a tree, no matter how much you are tempted to do so. They are living creatures who have been drawn to the same site as you have: you have no right to deny them what you yourself seek.

You may experience feelings you don't understand or are uncertain of. Always remember that you are in control. If you're not sure that you want to do something, don't do it.

If you are drawn to visit another site, by all means go and explore but do not meditate there: the different sensations may confuse you. For now you need to work with just one site.

Working with these sacred sites is at the very centre of all the spiritual practices outlined in the book. To the Celts the relationship between nature, the person and the spirit world was a central part of their life experience. To us it is new and unfamiliar; for them it was ancient and part of the clan history. It was how they were brought up, how they made sense of the worlds around them and how they lived their lives. To appreciate that, and share in even just a small part of it, is one of the most magical moments you will experience in your life. So, proceed slowly and savour every glorious moment.

5

USING YOUR INTUITION

We all have intuition, whether we choose to use it or not. Most people elect not to because they are cut off from the influences of the natural and spiritual world that help to magnify and intensify it to the point at which it is difficult to ignore. In the modern world, where everything is regimented, organised and packaged, it isn't possible to phone your boss and explain that you can't come to work today because you know intuitively that you must visit a sacred site. Imagine trying to persuade a neighbour not to plant a tree in a particular spot because you know intuitively that it would prefer to be planted with other trees in the nearby wood. It isn't easy to marry an inner knowledge that works to its own rhythms with our modern world but it is something you have to try to do.

In this chapter we are going to explore the nature of intuition and try some exercises to enhance your awareness of it. We will also look at how nature and the animal kingdom can help us increase our experience and understanding of it.

WHAT IS INTUITION?

During my morning walk with my dog, I cross the burn several times. One spot where I cross was shown to me in a dream as the place where I should wash and recharge my crystals. One day on my way there I picked up a small piece of quartz that was lying at the side of the track. When I reached the crossing point, I remembered that it was in my pocket and dropped it into the water.

Afterwards I wondered about my actions and realised that I had acted intuitively. I had made no conscious decision to pick up the quartz. I had just done it. I had had no plan for what to do with it: that, too, had just happened. Now I do *this* every time I go to the river and even ask an indulgence of the spirits of the site to ensure my safe return. This may seem rather fanciful but consider two things: first, there is a long tradition of paying tokens to spirits as you cross water. Look at any water feature in a modern airport and you will find that people still give tokens before a journey. Second, I have seen a spirit guardian at that site and felt his presence several times, so on the first occasion I had picked up something special about that spot and honoured it, without even being aware that I was doing so.

Essentially this is what intuition is: it is a method of enriching our lives and making us more aware of the world around us and our role in it. Once when we were staying at Applecross in the West Highlands and were out walking along a well-marked path, I suddenly felt a strong urge to veer off to the right through some trees. Nervous of the lie of the land, I resisted. But the pull strengthened, demanding my attention. Eventually I had to turn back and find the imagined track. Sure enough, there was a path and we followed it until it came out on the crest of a small hill with a stunning view south along the coast and out to the Hebrides. I thanked my intuition for leading me there.

Then I noticed a tent pitched way down below in an isolated bay and again the urge was upon me. This time I resisted it, arguing that we hadn't time to weave our way down there, but for the rest of the walk I had to fight the inclination to go and find the person in that tent. Who knows what I might have found out, or what doors that trip would have opened? Now I feel a sadness that I didn't follow my intuition and I'm certain if it happened again I would act on it.

There are, broadly, two schools of thought among those who try to explain intuition. The first is that it is merely a manifestation of our subconscious: when I found the path, I had already noticed it out of the corner of my eye, and while my conscious mind had paid it no attention, my subconscious had thought it worth exploring, perhaps remembering a similar path in the past that had yielded something interesting. Maybe I'd even heard someone mention it. The spectacular view was a bonus, although my subconscious mind might have hoped for it, given that we weren't far from the coast and the path was heading upwards.

As for the person in the tent, anyone camping on their own near one of Scotland's most important Celtic Christian sites is almost inevitably going to be on a spiritual quest and therefore worth talking to. Perhaps the tent reminded me of African explorers or maybe it was just the romanticism of a mysterious stranger. Who knows? The point is that it can all be explained quite reasonably like that.

The alternative view holds that intuition is not so easily defined. Rather, it is something much deeper, embedded in our very soul, that sometimes reaches out and guides us in ways that are mysterious to us. Intuition may use senses that we are only dimly aware of, senses that recognise the flow of energies and spirits around us. Like radar, it may sense danger and guide us to safety. It may sense kindred spirits and urge us to rendezvous with them. That might have been what happened on my walk. The sceptic might ask, Why doesn't intuition simply tell us this? The answer may be that the part of the brain connected with intuition is its right side, while language and writing are associated with the left. Perhaps for intuition to communicate with us, it has to speak directly to us, bypassing what the Brazilian author Paulo Coelho called the 'front brain' and using emotion and imagery, because they are the only means it has at its disposal.

While many people have tried to define intuition and academics have written many learned tomes on it, I feel that it is the inner knowledge that something is better for you than whatever the alternative seems to be. We are all following a spiritual path and when we choose an option that moves us along the path, we feel good and know within ourselves that it was the right choice. When we make a choice that moves us away from the path, it feels less good and, deep inside, we know it isn't right.

Many people think that intuition is some kind of psychic tool. Nothing could be further from the truth: intuition is a purely internal sense that applies only to you. Normally you cannot even communicate with your own intuition; the best you can hope for is to recognise its message and importance in your life.

IMPROVING OUR INTUITION

To improve our intuition we must listen to our inner intuitive urgings. To do this, we need to learn the techniques to hear them and also to magnify them to the point at which we can't ignore them.

The Celts lived their whole lives by this form of decision-making. They believed it was the Gods and Goddesses speaking to them, urging them to follow the flow of the energies of the land and destiny, and to be part of the bigger picture. They seem to have been so in tune with the seasons of the year and the flow of the land that it was impossible for them to ignore their intuitive urges.

Listening To Our Intuition

For this exercise you will need your journal or a separate notebook, if you prefer. It is often said that your body knows better than your mind what you need to eat. With this exercise we are going to test that.

Make your sign for opening a spiritual exercise. You can do either the Meditation Exercise or the Sitting Simply exercise. When you have emptied your mind, visualise going to the place where you normally eat – it may be a kitchen table or a chair in front of the television. There, all laid out, is a large silver dome covering your plate. You know that when you lift up the dome the food will be exactly what you need, what your body wants. Pause for a second. Now reach out and lift the lid. Look at what's on the plate. As you do so, you will realise that, yes, this is exactly what you want to eat.

Now put back the dome and turn away. Take time to become aware of your surroundings and when you are ready, make your sign of closure and open your eyes.

The whole point here is that very often we eat from habit, we tend to eat at the same times every day whether we want to or not. Even our choice of the kind of meals we prepare tends to be limited. How often have you sat down to a huge plate of pasta and thought wistfully of a small mixed salad? It happens so often to most of us and often because we have neglected our intuition. We knew what we wanted to eat but the practical part of our mind argued that we always had a large meal at that time of day.

Try to do this exercise before every meal, but at least once a day. Log what you wanted, what you actually ate and how you felt afterwards. Your entries might look something like this:

MONDAY 14TH
BREAKFAST
   vision: fresh fruit salad
   actual: cornflakes with banana
   feeling afterwards: okay, a little stuffed

LUNCH
   vision: green salad with pitta bread
   actual: two pre-packed hummus sandwiches, apple, piece of
      gingerbread
   feeling afterwards: still hungry and, paradoxically, a little sick.
      Very sleepy mid-afternoon

DINNER
   vision: potatoes, bean stew, carrots, followed by baked apple
   actual: pasta with pesto
   feeling: disappointed; food was insubstantial; snacked all night
      afterwards

In this case, I didn't eat anything my body was asking for. If I had, I probably wouldn't have been dozy in the afternoon and unsatisfied at night.

This is definitely an exercise to work on: it is amazing how rarely we listen to our intuition on these matters, but when we do it is equally startling how well we feel for it. Perhaps sometimes you can plan deliberately to follow your intuition, just to see how you feel afterwards.

Once you feel comfortable with this exercise, expand it into other areas of your life. Use it to ask yourself what you want to wear in the morning. Choosing clothes, especially for work, tends to become tedious and repetitive, yet we know that when we take time to dress as we want, we feel good. Use your intuition at first to consider what colours to wear, then what style – formal or casual.

Try this exercise to determine how to spend your spare time. Instead of slumping in front of the television, try to visualise what you *feel* like doing. Perhaps you will want to go for a walk, read a book, call friends, take up a hobby. Again, note what you actually did and how you felt about it.

Eventually you can expand this exercise into every facet of your life – your home, your work, your relationships. It can be frightening sometimes but also extraordinarily enlightening. Often you will exclaim, 'I knew that!' So, I would ask, why did you do nothing about it until now?

As you are trying to develop and integrate intuition into your life, you can deliberately provoke it. Create as many situations as possible where there is choice, then wait for intuition to tell you what to do. Do this as often as possible each day. Keep several different kinds of breakfast cereal in the house. Travel to work by different routes; use some form of transport, or walk. Do different things at lunchtime. With a little thought, you can build hundreds of choices into your daily life to the point that you will do it without even noticing, and that is when intuition works best.

Intuitive Mapping
This exercise is not only excellent for training yourself to trust your intuition, it is also immensely practical.

Choose a place you know that is not far away from where

you are now. Make your sign for opening a spiritual exercise, then do either your Meditation Exercise or the Sitting Simply exercise. When you have emptied your mind, visualise this place, then see how you would get there from where you are now. Imagine yourself getting into the car, or on to a bus, or whatever. See the roads you would travel down, the junctions you would cross. See the houses you would pass, or the factories. Look around, and take in as much detail as possible.

When you get to where you are going, look about and notice as much as possible. When you are ready, slowly return to where you are now. Count down from five, open your eyes and make your sign of closure.

Repeat this exercise until it is second nature to you. You need to recognise how you feel when you are imagining the route, and the sense of achievement when you arrive at your different destinations.

Gradually change the type of places you select. Choose locations you aren't as certain how to get to – somewhere you were once driven to by a friend, or you haven't been to for years. You may want to make the actual journey you imagined just to see how accurate the imagined version was.

Eventually choose places you haven't been to – a hotel or shop you notice in the local paper or an unfamiliar tourist attraction.

An alternative version of this exercise is to go to a strange town and try to find a particular kind of shop, or local landmark without using a map. You'll be amazed by how easy it is. The only time I get lost now is when I *do* use a map!

USING YOUR INTUITION

These exercises are valuable in awakening your innate ability to listen to and react to your intuition. This is of crucial importance as you develop your own spiritual practices and understandings: you must be able to trust your intuition. If you are walking along a path and suddenly feel a strong desire to clamber up a fern-clad bank, you need to be able to recognise and act on that intuition.

Where intuition comes into its own is in the discovery of sacred sites and what to do once you get there. Remember, your intuition is more than you: it accesses the flows and senses of the land around you. If you have the urge to take a particular route when approaching a sacred site, do so, and understand that this is, in some way, an important part of the whole ceremony.

When you are at a site you need to be aware of what you are doing and how you feel as you do it. Be open to sudden ideas, and be prepared to change your plans. One site I go to is a natural hollow in the ground that measures perhaps a hundred feet by fifty. It is easy to feel the gathering of men there, hidden from prying eyes. There are some stones that were once, perhaps, an altar: I had been using them for that purpose – but it never seemed right. One day it dawned me that what I was doing was wrong, and as I became aware of this, I knew what I needed to do. I moved my altar about ten feet. Now it feels fine.

You should not expect dramatic results. The changes you make may have no obvious purpose, but be sure that there is a reason, and be happy that you have been able to play some small part in a greater master plan.

LEARNING TO TRUST YOUR INTUITION

The main problem that most people cite when discussing intuition is that they lack faith in their urges. This is not surprising: we have been brought up in the Great Scientific Age where everything can be proved with an equation and laboratory experiment. Intuition, however, by its very nature, is unscientific. If we decide to pick some particular wood to burn in a bonfire and someone stops us and asks why we must use this wood, not branches from another dead tree nearer home, we cannot prove that this wood is more suitable. We just know it is.

The greatest barrier to intuition is common sense: it is rational, scientific and thus inappropriate. You must suspend it and go with what feels right. Once, in a city, I could not find a building I was looking for. It took me a while to realise that I was imposing common sense on my intuition: while my urge was to go one way, common sense said, 'No,' and gave all sorts of sensible reasons as to why I should go the other. Eventually I recognised what was happening, turned off my common sense and, within a couple of minutes, had found the place.

Don't think that if you could only follow your intuition all the time, to the exclusion of all else that is going on around you, everything would be perfect. That is not so. Remember that intuition is an inner awareness of subtle energies that surround and flow through us. That is all. For example, if I intuitively choose one path over another, then come across a landslide, slip and twist my ankle, you might wonder if my intuition was wrong. However, it might be that one path was surrounded by ash trees, the other by rowan, and my intuition realised that I would be inspired by the vivid red rowan berries. Intuitive awareness is not a psychic skill, it is a self-discovery tool. Keep that in mind. There may be occasions when your intuition will suggest actions that are plain dangerous and you have to say to yourself, 'Yes, that might be appropriate for me but I am not going to do it.' For example, walking in the dark through a strange town or seeking to meditate in a park that happens to be busy with schoolchildren might be intuitively attractive but just not practical.

Learning to trust your intuition becomes a lot easier when you recognise these problems and address them. Your intuition will not tell you to give up your job, leave the parental home or move house. What it will do is give you strong urges to spend more time creatively, on your own or in another type of location. How you react to your urges is up to you.

You might want to consider other things that are happening in your life, dreams, for example, or the sudden appearance of a friend you haven't seen for a while. It might be that someone gives you a book about Australia just after you've dreamed of walking in a desert or outback and intuitively you crave wide-open spaces and empty plains. Clearly you are receiving a message. It might not be possible to visit Australia, but you could find other, equally open spaces, read more books or watch films about the country. You could explore Aboriginal music and legends.

You might find you have particularly strong urges to visit your sacred site at particular times. Make a note of them, then see if they form any pattern: they may relate to phases of the moon, types of weather or cloud cover. One of my sites summons me when the East Lothian haar comes in. I've only been there once and I spent most of the time convinced that I was not in the same world!

USING ANIMALS TO UNDERSTAND OUR INTUITION

Birds and animals have long been recognised by the Celts as useful tools in understanding our intuition. Animals, with their simpler understanding, grasp quickly what needs to be done, what path should be taken, while we worry about the consequences of an action.

When St Samson was ordained a deacon in the sixth century in Wales, a wild dove flew in and sat on his shoulder. Only the two ministers – Bishop Dubricius and St Illtyd – saw it and professed it to be a blessing from the Divine Spirit. Celtic saints often presented the Holy Spirit as a dove, and also as a wild goose. Both birds were seen to encapsulate the relationship to nature and independence of spirit necessary to follow a spiritual life.

The belief that you are working with the flows of energy in the land is a key element in using intuition. It is easier to swim with the tide than against it and as long as we know where we are going all will be well. Often, however, it isn't easy to read the land or be aware of its energy.

Animals can help in this. We have a cat, and often when we go for walks at night, he will come with us. But he has his territory, and when we walk beyond his frontiers, he will not follow. Indeed, he will sit and miaow, sounding quite distressed, until we return. In other parts of his patch the boundaries seem more fluid: sometimes he will come with us, sometimes not. I didn't understand this until one day I explored his frontier and realised that I could sense a territorial end, almost like a barrier. I would not have noticed it without the cat. Indeed, thinking about it now, the road, which goes straight on, used to bend at ninety degrees in this spot as it approached an ancient bridge that crossed the river.

Dogs are also sensitive to intuition. They choose some paths and trails over others. My old terrier would sit facing due east with me and meditate; she could sense the nature of a site and I always used her as a judge of whether or not there was any danger. If a dog or cat is uncomfortable in a location, it is better avoided.

Birds can also be a good guide to the mood of the land energies. If they are loud and fluttering or swooping low over the ground, you are not in a restful place. If, on the other hand, they soar on the updraughts and glide high over the fields then you are in a good place. I have even known birds to fly in front and behind me, pushing me forward.

You need to build intuitive awareness of all of this, sense what the ambience is and react accordingly. If when you sit to meditate, your cat distracts you, try to understand why that is. Of course, it may always do so when you sit down, but if it only does it when you are preparing to meditate, something may not be right with either the place or the way you are going about it. Are you using opening and closing ceremonies? Do you need to seal the room for added empowerment? These are questions that only you can answer. But finding the answer will validate your intuition and lead to more complete and rewarding spiritual practice.

Intuition, then, far from being a strange psychic gift, is a very practical tool for improving your spiritual practice. Indeed, it is an essential tool. Without it you can read the books and do the exercises, but you cannot understand and respond to the subtleties of the land, the flow of the energies, the urgings of the spirits and truly learn to walk the mist.

6

WORKING WITH THE SPIRIT REALMS

St Mary's Kirk is ruined church on the bleak north coast of Caithness about six miles west of Thurso. It is reached by an overgrown footpath, which takes you across a wide strath, complete with highland stream and old abandoned mill, then climbs up the sandy dunes to reach this most windswept and desolate of spots. The current ruin dates from the twelfth century although the site is without doubt much older. It features an eternal spring and the church is set back – just a little too much – from the grass-tufted cliffs.

But it's there. You can sense it as you approach. The air seems to thicken, and even through the decay and abandonment, the magic sparkles. I feel it as a single shiver that runs up my back and makes my scalp tingle in delight. My heart lightens and my soul sings out. And at St Mary's, its cries are answered. For this is one of those most precious sites where spirits seem to congregate; where the air is thick with them. And simply to be there is to share a fraction of their strange contentment and restless urging.

The Celts, as I have already said, made no distinction between the material and spiritual world. To understand something was to comprehend both its physical and spiritual aspects. Trees were worshipped not only for their age and beauty but also because they were powerful beings and because they attracted spirits. Crystals, quartz crystal especially, were venerated for the same reasons.

The Celts recognised that we ourselves are surrounded by spirits. In later times the Celtic monks talked about heavenly choirs of angels, and it seems that angels were ever present to undertake the most mundane tasks: in the mid sixth century the ever forgetful St Aeden was dispatched to Ireland and forgot to take his 'dear little bell', a parting gift from St David. The latter, knowing that his disciple would be distraught to have left it behind, despatched it to him with an angel who flew across the Irish Sea until he reached the young monk in his small boat.

The writers of such tales took for granted the choirs of angels, as Rhygyfarch's *Life of St David*, written in 1081 indicates. It was as if there were angels across the land working with and watching over the great Celtic saints.

THE NATURE OF THE SPIRITUAL REALMS

There are many problems in trying to understand the world of the spirits. The first is that it is so different from our world that we have little to hang on to as a reference point when we try to describe it or understand what it is like. Imagine a world where there is no need for food or clothing, or even a body. Imagine a place where there is no longer greed, ambition or lust. It leaves you almost breathless with incomprehension. And this means that when we do make contact, however fleeting, we are even more confused.

A second problem with spirits is that we tend to impose on their world our ideas of how things work. We think of hierarchies, of rules and obligations; systems and strata; directors and workers. This is odd because many of us actually believe that in a perfect world there would be no need for any government, rules or restrictions because we would all be so enlightened that we would never seek to cheat or steal. We think this of our world but still believe that spirits and angels must have some rigid definition of duty with penalties for disobedience.

My own experiences have allowed me to make some attempt at understanding the Otherworld. As at St Mary's, I can often say that I've sensed spirits around me. Occasionally they materialise. One Samhain I was collecting dried-up silver birch branches from a site I visit a lot. While I was snapping the old wood into small, even-sized lengths, I froze with the certainty that I was being watched. Slowly I looked up. Standing ahead of me was an old man, completely in white, even his complexion. He was wearing heavy robes with complex Celtic designs picked out in the stitching on the long sleeves that hung down from his crossed arms.

I dropped the firewood. He stared at me apparently waiting for something. Eventually I stuttered, 'Bloody hell, I can see you.' And so I could, as clear as day. This was no shadow or play of light. The trees behind him were blocked out by him – he was definitely there.

He spoke to me with a message that made no sense but which I noted down later as best I could. He called me by a name that is not mine and my sense was that the language he spoke was not English, though it reached me as that. Since then I've seen him a couple of times and we have never communicated. Not too profound, but life-changing for me: before, I had always felt that a lot of what I took to be spiritual happenings were no more than my over-fertile imagination.

Now I believe. The spirits we see are those which are still tied to the material earth plane. They seem to be attracted to the energies of a site and are so entranced with the material world that they can cross through the veil between the worlds relatively easily. In my experience, they are the ones who have little interest in us as developing spiritual beings. For me, the main role that they have played is to reaffirm that the spiritual dimension really does exist.

Then there are spirits like angels who take form and meddle in our affairs but are not attached to any one site, although they may be attached to humans. Among them are almost certainly the spirits of our ancestors and extended soul family who seek to help and guide us along our spiritual path.

There is a third type of spirit that does not take form. While these spirits maintain a link with the earth plane, it is much less strong and much less important to them. At places like St Mary's, however, they find the energy of that site attractive and flock there.

We can speculate that there might be other levels for spirits who do not take form and have turned their backs on the material world altogether.

One category I have not listed here is faeries: the Tuatha dé Danaan have their own story to tell and we will deal with it later.

There are are lots of categories of 'little folk' – Scottish faeries, elves, light-beings, brownies, etc. It isn't clear how they fit into the categorisation outlined above. It may be that they are forms of spirits so attached to the earth plane that they tend it and look after it, like gardeners. Equally they may be on a different evolutionary plan altogether.

HOW DO WE EXPLAIN THIS?

We have no way of knowing what the Druids believed or taught and it would be wrong to suggest otherwise. However, if we assume that the Celtic monks were teaching something similar then we can turn to those texts. Here we find many references to the Gospel of St John. Indeed, some would argue that the Celtic Christian Church was founded on the teachings of St John while the Roman church was founded on those of St Peter. The teachings of St John came to the Celts from the Coptic Church in Egypt, whose understandings were modelled on the Gnostic and Zoroastrian pre-Christian teachings.

Basically the Gnostics taught that understanding was only revealed in stages as you were ready to cope with the consequences of that knowledge. It was said that in the great temple of Alexandria there existed an original copy of the Gospel of St John, whose teachings were so controversial that they could only be shown to the truly enlightened leaders of the Church.

Abbot George Burke, of the Gnostic Orthodox Church in the

USA, revealed that one of his reasons for leaving the Eastern Orthodox monastery he belonged to was that the monks were taught of the eternal nature of the soul, which lived many lives and ultimately returned to the Godhead, while the laity were taught that there was only one life, and then either heaven or hell for ever.

The Copts thought that the gaining of knowledge over many lifetimes, and through all sorts of experiences, makes us more compassionate and more aware that our actions have consequences that can enhance or harm others. They argued that as this understanding grows so our spiritual awareness expands. As we seek to lead a more compassionate and meaningful life, we cease to crave material comforts and distractions.

We become aware of the spiritual dimensions and start to explore and develop our understanding of them. Our eyes turn away from material fripperies and we seek spiritual fulfilment and commitment. As we are reborn, life after life, we then slowly move from material-world rebirth to spiritual rebirth. And so Gnostics would argue that the spirits we meet are simply more spiritually advanced souls. And, being more advanced, they want to help us develop.

The ultimate goal is our return to the Godhead, where we all came from and where we all will ultimately return. As we reject the material world like a rocket leaving the earth's orbit, our attention switches to the faraway sun glowing benignly and calling to us.

This is the Godhead. I do not call it 'God', because the concept of 'God' has too many associations with a white man in a white robe on a white cloud. We are talking here about something much less human. The Godhead is not an active force, it simply *is*. There is no point in praying to the Godhead for help in finding a lost earring or even ending a war, for the Godhead is passive. This can be difficult for some people to accept but the more I think about it the more it seems right to me.

CELTIC ANGELS AND SPIRITS

The Celts knew that we can call on a whole host of spirits for aid and support. If you're a Christian, or from a Christian background, you may see them as guardian angels; if you are not Christian you may see them as spirits.

From our modern twenty-first-century viewpoint, it can be rather disconcerting to think of spirits being with us all the time, whether we are making love or shouting at our children. However, you must remember that these are not creatures of the material world and their feelings and concerns are not ours. I sometimes think it must be a little like our relationship with our pets where we care for them and clear up after them without embarrassment or resentment, and guide them away from danger and injury. The animals are not embarrassed or resentful about this either.

Several different kinds of spirit look after us. The first is our soul-friend, our special counsellor, to whom we can tell everything, confess all our sins, our failings and fears, and who can offer us wise advice and counsel.

Meeting Your Soul-friend

Before you go to sleep at night, do this visualisation exercise. You may need to do it for a few nights before you dream. And be aware that not all soul-friend spirits want to be seen. I have never seen mine, for example, though I think that is more down to me than any reluctance on his part. Also you need to know that the spirit will come to you in a form you find pleasing and non-threatening. You may dream of a grandmother-type figure, if that is pleasing to you, or of a fit, healthy man. The form in which they come to you is of no importance: it is for your benefit only. Once they have chosen of form they will not change it.

Before bed, have a shower or bath. Imagine all the impurities and dirt of the day washing away. Dress in natural fabrics and, if you can, put some alder wood beside your bed. Alder is the

*dreaming wood and it's dark groves contain many secrets wait-
ing to be beheld.*

*Once in bed, do not read or be distracted in any way. Lie down
and make the sign you use for opening spiritual work. Meditate
as you lie there. When you are floating, feel the safety and warmth
of your bed filling you with peace and contentment. See sleep as
a great gentle dark tunnel. As you drift towards it, imagine you
are on a boat floating slowly along the river in the summer warmth.
The heat of the day is still in the air and you smile in pure pleasure, perhaps even stretch out and squirm slightly in sheer delight.*

*Now you hear a second boat just behind you, gliding smoothly
along. You know your soul-friend is there. You can sense them
looking at you and smiling indulgently at your simple pleasure.
They like you to be contented and happy, and you are glad they
can see you like this.*

*You close your eyes and drift. You wonder if they'll say
anything. If they don't speak, you don't. You know that. And it
doesn't matter. It's just being with them that's so important. It's
so peaceful.*

*As sleep enfolds you, think of your soul-friend at your side
and let your dreams start with this. At this time of waking/sleep-
ing you are so open to their influence that later, you may not be
sure if what you dream actually happened.*

*If they wish it, you will meet your soul-friend, who may tell
you how to contact them in the future. Every soul-friend has
different ways and you need to listen carefully to what they say.
They may take you for a walk somewhere to show you something (or someone) special to you.*

*Remember that this is only the first time. You have the rest of
your life together so there is no need to rush anything. Take it
easy and enjoy.*

*When you wake in the morning remember to make your sign
to close down spiritual practice. Perhaps leave yourself a note
to remind you to do this. Also keep it in mind to write down
everything that happens. You might think that meeting your soul-*

friend spirit would be so important that it would be imprinted on your mind. In fact, it seems to slip away all too easily.

Once a conversation is underway, do not be afraid to ask your soul-friend questions, about yourself and your life and also about him- or herself. They are there to guide you towards fulfilling your life purpose, but it is rare that they will tell you explicitly what it is. You must learn to listen to them and trust them. Indeed, the first words I ever heard from my soul-friend were, 'Trust me.'

Once you have made this sort of contact, you will find it easier and easier to talk to your soul-friend and hear their replies. An easy way to do this is to keep a special candle for him or her: when you need to speak with them, sit in a quiet space and light the candle. Make the sign for starting spiritual work and then do the Meditation Exercise (see page 33). As you are floating, wait for them to appear to you either in your mind's eye, or in front of you.

Another way is to go for a walk: as you stroll along seek out your soul-friend's presence. You will feel as if someone is walking just behind your right shoulder. To me it feels like when your partner, or someone you know well is walking with you; you don't have to turn round to know where they are.

The second type of spirits whom the Celts believed worked with them are the ancestor spirits, family members who have died but whose spirits have remained to help future generations. They may not even be people you knew or had even heard of. As the traditional clan and extended family collapses and as people move about more and more, we know less and less about our biological ancestors.

Of course, these people might have had biological or emotional characteristics that you have inherited, so sometimes they are well placed to help you in your journey. Because the family was so important to the Celts, these spirits played a large part in their lives. They consulted them in all major decisions, and local Druids acted as intermediaries in interpreting what the spirits were saying, much as mediums do now.

Today we can access the knowledge of the ancestors more directly. Find out about your ancestors and look for someone that you admire or who you want to emulate. Perhaps someone reared a whole family to become well-adjusted adults, or someone who gave everything up to cycle across Australia. Once you find someone, try to get hold of one of their possessions. By holding it, as they held it, you can reach back to them.

Contacting the Ancestors

Make your sign to start spiritual work. Holding or touching your ancestor's object, sit in your sacred space and either do the Sitting Still exercise or the Meditation Exercise.

Now become aware of the object you are touching. Feel your ancestor beside you. Let them touch the object and, aloud, ask them about it. Listen to their reply. Ask them about their life and how they spent it. Remember that this kind of contact is probably strange for them too, and your questions may stir up memories that might be painful for them. But remember that they have chosen to be with you so they want to help you.

Do ask them questions, but don't probe too deeply. You may feel that you need to talk to them several times before you are confident enough to ask what you really want to know.

When you feel it is time to end the session, thank your ancestor for coming to you, then put down the object carefully. Now imagine a rain of pure white light cleansing you thoroughly. Feel the cold fresh energy rush through you and leave you invigorated. Now make the sign for ending spiritual work and take a couple of minutes to return to normal. Remember to write in your journal everything you can remember about the conversation.

The third group of spirits that are there to help us includes other members of our own soul family. These spirits share our soul, for each of us is not a complete soul on its own: we are part of larger families. This allows the collective soul to learn everything it needs to know and so progress faster towards the

Godhead. Each part of the collective soul is more or less independent but they all have to let go of the material world to continue the journey back to the Godhead.

These are the spirit guides I have used most. For me they do not take form; rather, they create emotions in me that tell me whether what I am doing is for the better or not. It is almost impossible to explain: it is just a sense that these feelings do not originate within me but are important. Generally I have the sense of having experienced something similar before, yet I know that can't be so. For example, I cannot go anywhere near the edge of cliffs no matter how high the fence or wide the path. It's not that I have vertigo, it's that the thought of jumping off is strangely alluring. Even while I am struggling to get away, I can feel the wind as it rushes past me, imagine the strange euphoria of flying and it is only the sudden realisation, as I plummet, that this was all a terrible mistake – that I didn't want to die after all that pulls me back. There's no pain, no horror, just these conflicting, sensations.

At first I thought this was my imagination and then I considered whether it was something from a past life. I am now fairly confident it is neither. I have no idea why I feel this desire to jump. I am certain, however, that someone from my soul family is helping me to break this strange, dangerous fascination. Several times now, it is only this most powerful sensation of helpless regret that has brought me to my senses.

Members of your soul family will be spread out all over the world in all cultures and all times. Such is the breadth of experience that the soul family seeks; there is nowhere it won't go, no experience it won't try. So there is a huge pool of knowledge for you to access. Learn to trust the sense within you that everything is as it should be.

If you have a trial of some kind, you can access your soul-family spirits to help you. To call to them, try the following exercise.

Calling Your Soul Family
Sit in your sacred space and make the sign for spiritual work.

Do the Sitting Still exercise. Now, once you are calm and feel open to the ebbs and flows of the spirit world all around you, take some paper and write a letter to your soul family, perhaps something like this:

> *Dear Soul Brothers and Sisters, I am writing to ask for your help. I know in all of our experiences we must have faced this problem a thousand times but I am tired and despondent because no solution seems apparent to me. I keep trying to find my spiritual path but when I glimpse it, I seem to lose it. Now I feel as if I am wandering in a wood of blackthorn, unable to find a way forward or back. My path seems lost. What can I do?*
>
> *My relationship with my partner is boring. My children have lives of their own and don't need me any more. I hate my job. Even my friends seem to have deserted me. What can I do?*

Hopefully your letter won't be so down hearted! Reread it a couple of times to make sure you have written exactly what you want to ask, then seal it in an envelope. To post it to your soul family, you must burn it, ideally in a bonfire. Put in some green leaves or grass cuttings so that when you throw the letter on to the fire, it creates a lot of smoke. As the smoke rises up and dissipates into the night, imagine your letter spreading out for all parts of your soul family to read.

Either through your dreams or meditation, you should receive a reply within a few days. If you hear nothing, do not despair: simply repeat the exercise. Sometimes we receive a reply but we do not realise it. It may not be as direct as someone talking to you. It may be something you hear on the radio, or a story someone tells you at work. All I can say is that normally you will know it when you hear it. And remember to thank your soul family for their help.

WORKING WITH LOCAL GODS AND GODDESSES

While spirits are all around us, the Celts believed that other guides were specific to certain places or had powers on which we could call for help in particular situations. These gods and goddesses are independent of us and while they are happy to help, they are not as personal to us as the spirits we have talked about so far. As most of these gods and goddesses were adopted by the Christian church, you can, if you prefer, work with them as saints.

You may live in an area where there are wishing wells and sacred springs. Try to find out more about them and visit them. Usually you will be expected to make some sort of gift: food or water; perhaps a token like a rag tied to a tree or a ribbon to a branch of a bush. If you are not sure, trust your intuition.

Certain sites are traditionally associated with particular cures and others with the bestowing of favours, like money, pregnancy or a new lover. Fewer sites are linked to particular entities, but where they are it is usually to a Celtic saint who will have used a previously pagan site. Where ancient churches stand on the tops of hills, for example, they are often dedicated to St Michael, a transformation of the pagan sea god Mannán mac Lir into a saint. He was also the god of messages – which were passed from hilltop to hilltop. This ancient association of St Michael with the sea explains the popularity of St Michael's Day among the fishing communities of the Western Isles. It was celebrated until the early twentieth century, with great festivals, the exchange of gifts and sporting competitions.

CELTIC GODS AND GODDESSES

The Celts respected local gods and we must assume that they were effective to attract veneration for hundreds, perhaps thousands, of years. Yet they were associated with only one site. There was no pantheon of Celtic gods and goddesses as there was in the Roman or Greek traditions. There was no Mount Olympus where the gods lived. That said, there were gods with similar attributes, which existed in different parts of the Celtic lands with different names and appearances. To work with them, either in their pre-Christian or Christian phase, you must first create a shrine.

Creating a Shrine

A shrine differs from an altar because it is dedicated to only one god or goddess. The five elements must be present: nature, fire, water, air and earth. Try to link them with the divinity to whom you are dedicating your shrine.

Find an image of the god or goddess to use as the centre point. Nowadays many shops sell such things or you can find them on the Internet. It will be, however, something highly personal to you. If someone you love buys it for you, you will have the emotional tie of their love to imbue the statue with even more emotion.

Add to the shrine other objects relevant to the God or Goddess. For example, if it is to Bridgid (see below), you may like to add some small pieces of artwork you have created yourself, perhaps especially for the shrine, or pictures of your children.

In front of the statue place two candles, one on each side, to create a triangle. When you sit in front of the shrine with the candles lit, see this triangle. See the energy flowing from the candles to the God or Goddess. Eventually you may be able to conjure up the image of a great hall in which the candles become burning braziers. See the high grey stone walls and the flagstone floors. Feel the veneration and power of this place. Walk forward slowly towards the dais at the end and, as you do, glance up and see the god or goddess there. They may or may not acknowledge you. Bow. In your hand you are holding a small candle. Place it on the bottom step of the dais and step back, keeping your head bowed all the time. Back away, stealing glances at the god or goddess as you do.

If you can, paint or sketch the god or goddess as you saw them and put the result on your shrine.

SOME CELTIC GODS AND GODDESSES

Bridgid

The earth mother. She is celebrated at Imbolc, 1 February, the celebration that occurs half-way between the winter solstice and the spring equinox. It is a celebration of the coming of spring, and while the worst of the winter may not be past, at least the end is in sight. It is a time for people to stir again: farmers in the fields, travellers on the road. Bridgid is also associated with creativity and motherhood. As St Bridgid she was midwife to the Virgin Mary, and there are many incarnations of her as a saint. She founded Kildare Monastery on the banks of the river Liffey west of Dublin.

Cernunnos

Portrayed as a tall young warrior with deer's antlers, Cernunnos is Lord of the Forest, King of the Animals. He is the nature god, and although there are few dedications to him, such was his popularity in Gaul that the Church in Europe had to portray him as Lucifer with cloven hoofs and spiked tail. His persecution marks the distancing of the Church from the forces of nature, a division unknown to the Celtic saints or their Gnostic forebears. Cernunnos stands for the natural untamed world, both in the land and in ourselves. He is the antidote to sanitised city life. Think of the noble stag running free in the Caledonian forests or the golden eagle high above the mountains of Wicklow. That is Cernunnos.

The Daghda

This is the male god. While Cernunnos is the young male in nature, the Daghda is the mature father figure. Often portrayed in a not-too-flattering light, he is fat, loud and powerful. He has a magic cauldron that never empties, a magic harp that plays itself and a huge club. He is the provider, the charmer and the protector; all, of course, aspects of the male.

Lugh

The great skillsman. He succeeded Nauda as King of the Tuatha dé Danaan, revealing the importance to the Celts of gaining skills. There is no trade that he had not mastered. At the Battle of Magh Tuireadh the Northern, he was deemed so valuable to the Tuatha dé Danaan that the gods tried to prevent him fighting by surrounding him with their own soldiers. However, he escaped and won the day for the Danaan by killing Balor, his grandfather, and driving the Fomorii back under the sea.

Aine

The goddess of healing, protection, fertility and prosperity. She was the daughter of Mannán mac Lir, god of the sea, and later, in Christian times, became known as the Queen of the Faeries. A fickle goddess, she would seek recompense from those who displeased her.

Aine is the goddess to appeal to over health matters. She gave her name to the vital spark that keeps a body alive. Among traditional healing circles and herbalists, she is often invoked to help medicines work and the body heal.

HAVING A RELATIONSHIP WITH A GOD OR GODDESS

While I would say that my patron is St Kessog and that I also work with other saints, my shrine is dedicated primarily to Cernunnos. When I first came across him, I was apprehensive. I was from a Christian background, and found it difficult to get past the Lucifer image, but two events changed my mind. The first was a bonfire we made for the winter solstice. We had built it about eight feet high, and as we gathered round it in the darkness, the red and orange flames leaped up the dry wood. In moments the fire was like a roaring furnace. To my amazement as it began to die down a figure emerged from it. We all saw a human shape with great antlers covered with flames. At first I felt fear, then exhilaration as I recognised Cernunnos.

After that I began to work a little with him. I was writing a novel set in fifth-century Ireland and without so much as an invite, Cernunnos became a character in it. At first I was determined this wasn't to be but as the story developed he became more and more important to the plot. And as this happened the story I was telling became increasingly real to me. It felt right. It felt good. And so I let Cernunnos stay.

Working with Cernunnos, I feel, is also a reaction against certain factions who tell us that untamed nature is a spiritual danger to us. That somehow we need to fear everything that is not urbanised, domesticated and controlled. This, of course, is something I feel we should reject.

Use the gods on your shrine when you want to work with whatever they represent. If you are frustrated at lack of progress at work, or resent barriers and petty bureaucracy you have to face, bring the Daghda to your shrine. Draw a picture of him or perhaps find a photo of the Cerne Abbas Giant, a huge figure outlined in white chalk on a hill in Dorset. Each day sit with that drawing or photo and study it; try to imagine what it would be like to be the Dagdha – full of energy, eager for battle and confident of victory. Imagine striding through the office and daring anyone to challenge you. Make it happen for you.

As we walk the mist, seeking our path of spiritual progress, the spirits and gods that surround us can help us to put the events of the material world into perspective and to show us how inspiring and beautiful the spiritual world is. They want us to succeed, they want us to grow and understand more about the world around us. Let them into your life and take that step forward.

7

GOING ON A PILGRIMAGE

For most of us today, going on a pilgrimage suggests months away from home, struggling across inhospitable deserts or rocky mountaintops. We tend to think of medieval merchants and princes travelling, possibly in some comfort, to Canterbury, New Age writers like Shirley Maclaine on el Camino across northern Spain to Santiago de Compostela, or millions of Muslims replicating the actions of the Prophet on the Hajj to Mecca. Each year millions of people across the world take part in organised and personal pilgrimages. Whether they go to Lourdes, Rome, Jerusalem, Mecca, Mount Kamji or Kataragama in Sri Lanka, these people are recognising the power of the sites.

People go on pilgrimage for many reasons, some to pray for forgiveness or to atone for sins they believe they have committed. Others seek help for loved ones or want to show their devotion. Whatever the reason, there is some deeply held sense that pilgrimage is good for the soul.

But pilgrimage is far more than simply undertaking a task in order to gain favour with our Gods. Primarily, it is about stepping out of our everyday life to immerse ourselves in another, more basic form of living where every day our ambition is just to reach to the next point on the way. It shows that the only things that matter are food, shelter, safety and health. If you grasp that fact and acknowledge it, you will be able to reflect on your own life and get problems into perspective. A pilgrimage, then, like a true holiday, allows you to return refreshed and renewed, able to appreciate your blessings and cope better with the trials of your life.

For most people their route and destination can be said hardly to matter: it is the journeying that is important. In that sense a pilgrimage need be little more than a stroll round the park. Sufis, Hindus and Buddhists all seem to have recognised this and although there are pilgrimage sites associated with these religions, there are also many retreat centres that encourage guests to begin an inner journey while in a supportive environment.

For the Celt the latter form of pilgrimage seems to have been the most popular. While there are pilgrim routes in the Celtic lands, there is no evidence that any predate the widespread blossoming of the pilgrimage routes in the early part of the last millennium. Indeed, many of the most popular ones, Glastonbury Abbey and St Andrews, for example, seem to have been created more for the revenue that the pilgrims brought rather than any religious reason.

When the Celts went on pilgrimage they seem to have taken aimless walks. In the ninth century *Voyage of St Brendan* we are told that the Celtic saint set off for the mystical island where heaven met earth with no more than prayers to God and a fully provisioned ship, no map, no plan, no pilot.

Similarly, retreat centres were common in Celtic lands. These were called *culdees* and operated like monasteries with small permanent communities whose numbers were swelled by others who would spend a couple of days there each week. *Culdees* existed in Scotland until at least the eleventh century.

A Celtic pilgrimage, then, is a walk without destination or plan. It is the travelling that is important and it can be as long or as short as you want. It can be an arduous climb across the mountains, or a stroll along the beach. You can fast on water and bread or you can feast on fresh fruit and salads. The choice is yours.

The difference between a pilgrimage and a long walk is the attitude of the pilgrim. Some sing as they go, or chant. Almost all wear something to identify themselves as pilgrims.

For the Celt the point of the pilgrimage was to be submerged in the world of nature and spirit, to leave the material world far behind. You may start off by seeking answers to questions, or guidance and help. But the pilgrimage takes you instead to another place where tranquillity and calm can heal, sooth and inspire you.

CELTIC PILGRIMAGE

For the Celt, a walk through the woods was a spiritual act: it brought you into contact with spirits who were connected to the trees or the woodland animals and birds. Think of all the thousands of different creatures you would come across in a wood – animals, plants, trees, insects, birds, bushes, weeds and so much more. Reach out to connect with their spirits and think of all the stimulation you would enjoy in something so simple.

Now think of how it would feel if all these spirits were trying to help you. Think how they could lift you out of the material world and help you fly in the world of the spirits. Imagine leaving behind all your cares and worries and floating peacefully in a world where angels and spirits tend you and show you the folly of our world and the wonder of theirs. Imagine the joy you would feel.

Pilgrimage Meditation
In your Sacred Space look around and notice the four elements and the nature surrounding you. Make your sign for starting spiritual work. Now do the Sitting Simply or Meditation Exercise.

You are now standing at the start of a long, straight track and crowding in on both sides are tall green trees. You can see bright sunshine dappling their topmost leaves and the air is heavy with the sweet contentment of a hot summer's day.

Now begin to walk along this track. As you do, you will begin to feel happier. Now you are smiling. All around, you can sense small animals and birds dozing in the heat. You can feel the spirits in the trees watching you and smiling. They are happy and content, and that sense of well-being rubs off on you.

You stretch out both your arms and now you can actually feel the mass of spirits all around you. The air seems thicker, and you feel supported and cared for. You let the spirits guide you. Now you are floating a foot or so above the track. Each step you take seems to go on for ever. You could fly to the ends of the world. It feels so good to be free.

Now the spirits bring you back to the ground. You thank them for their help. Now just stand and be yourself once again. Slowly become aware of your fingers, your toes, where you are. Open your eyes. Make your sign for finishing spiritual work.

The experience of a Celtic pilgrimage is different from visiting a sacred site because you are not focusing on any one spot and how it can help you meditate; rather, you are grazing on many sites as you walk, opening your mind to the subtle images that surround us all the time. It is a change in awareness. Normally in our day-to-day life we are almost totally focused on our internal thoughts and worries. How often have you walked, or even driven, to town and been unable to remember passing a particular landmark or road crossing? This is a serious blocking of awareness: we use too much processing space for worries and not enough for enjoyment of the amazing world of nature that surrounds us. So, a Celtic pilgrimage is a walk into awareness.

PREPARING FOR A PILGRIMAGE

The first thing to do is allocate the time for it. Try to set aside a full day, but failing that as long as you can manage. You don't want to have to watch the time while you are on pilgrimage as this would spoil your ability to enjoy and appreciate the experience. Later, you should plan for a pilgrimage to last several days. There can be few more spiritually rewarding achievements than reconnecting with nature through long periods spent in the dramatic splendour of the Scottish Highlands or the gentle uplands of southern Ireland.

Even for a one-day pilgrimage, I plan well ahead, trying to set aside one day a month. Usually the date will come to me while I am meditating. If you have a busy, timetabled life it may not be possible for you to escape when your spirits want you to, and if that is so, you will just have to ring fence a day or half a day a couple of weeks ahead and let everyone know that this is your special time.

When the day arrives don't be put off by the weather. It is too easy to argue that it's too hot, too cold, too wet, too windy or any one of a hundred other excuses. Once you are out, you'll love it. Obviously, you need to use your common sense: if a blizzard is blowing on your date you will just have to spend the day inside 'on retreat' instead.

Next, decide where to go. As a Celtic pilgrimage is not aimed at any one place, you only need to establish the general direction. Again, meditation or Sitting Simply will help you choose. You should go somewhere in nature, preferably where you will not meet other people.

Often I will have a rough idea of where I am heading. For example, near to where I live there is a stone called the Witches' Cairn. I've lost count of the number of times I've set off on a pilgrimage with a vague idea of heading to that spot and I've yet to reach it. I get so far, then discover a glen I've never explored or a strange shape on the side of a hill that leads me off into higher areas. Once I simply missed a turning off the path I was on. But every day out has been successful and rewarding.

Of course, many people may feel uncomfortable about going out without an end in mind. If that is the case, you may prefer, at least for the first few times, to find a local site of pilgrimage. Traditionally pilgrimages are seen as a homage to important religious sites and you may want to choose an old church or the ruin of an abbey or monastery as your first target. Alternatively find somewhere that feels significant for you; a hilltop, or a cave, or perhaps some standing stones.

If you are lucky there may even be local pilgrimage trails. Increasingly these are being renewed and developed because of the current interest in hill-walking and rediscovering local history. To walk an ancient pilgrimage trail is something very special. Even if you do not share the religious beliefs of the original pilgrims, you can enjoy the sense of history and reverence for the adventure, the comradeship of centuries of similar pilgrims.

You could buy an Ordnance Survey map and look for trails marked in the countryside. We live on the edge of a wilderness so I often choose a point on the map and set off, uncertain where I'll end up. Despite being intuitive travellers, it is a good idea to take a map and compass with you. Just in case.

You could also close your eyes, ask your guides for help, then stick a pin into a map. That will give you a target and you will need to work out how to get to it. However, as it will be a Celtic pilgrimage, don't worry about whether or not you'll reach the spot: use your intuition to decide where to start from, you will be guided to experience what is required.

To go on a pilgrimage is to undertake not only a geographic journey, it is to follow internal paths as well. For this reason it is best undertaken alone as others may distract or annoy you. If you prefer to travel with others, set down some ground rules before you leave. Broadly, you should ensure that if anyone feels the need for a rest or to explore a particular spot, they can. Decide in advance how this can be achieved without hindering the rest of the group.

On the day of the pilgrimage, let someone know where you are going and when you expect to return. All the rules of hill-walking apply. Don't think that because you're only going a few miles you can afford to ignore them – you only have to slip and twist an ankle for a stroll in the hills to become a matter of life and death.

I always fast while on pilgrimage. It wasn't a conscious decision, I just came to recognise that I didn't want to eat and, if

I did, it felt wrong. However, I still take some food with me in case I need it. Better safe than sorry.

ON YOUR WALK

First, leave behind your day-to-day worries. You may wish to meditate before you set off and also to spend some time anticipating your walk. Once you step out of your house or your car focus on something – a tree or plant, perhaps – and spend some time examining it, really seeing it. Don't forget to consider its spiritual aspect. Or you may prefer to imagine walking through a shower of white light: as you pass through it all your daily cares and responsibilities are washed away. You step on cleansed and freed, ready for the pilgrimage.

Walk for about a minute, then stop. Look around you. See the trees and the bushes; see the grass and the small stones under your feet; feel the breeze on your face and the heat of the sun; smell the scents of the day, bend and touch the ground, feeling the texture of the earth. This will remind you to keep in touch with nature, which is all around you. Try to stop every fifteen minutes or so and remind yourself of this; use all your senses to rediscover nature and be alert to it all the time.

Traditionally pilgrims went barefoot. Even King James IV approached Whithorn in Galloway in this manner. Of course, this was easier when most people had no shoes and feet were hardier than they are now. I normally try to walk barefoot for some of the time, perhaps over a field or meadow or on a sandy beach. The rest of the time I wear hiking boots. But if you can walk barefoot, so much the better.

Be aware of how you move. Think about how your feet touch the earth. Are you walking slowly and gently, considerate and kind? Or are you marching along the track, purposefully taking control? Relax. It isn't a race. What terrible thing will happen if you only manage a fraction of the route you had planned?

Try to connect on a spiritual level with the land. Be aware that you are surrounded by spirits all the time. Try to acknowledge them. Remember the Pilgrimage Meditation and try to re-create it as you walk. If you are drawn to a particular spot, stop and enjoy the view. Try to see as much of the life around you as you can. You'll be amazed at the flowers you would have missed if you had been striding along, the insects busy in their own wee worlds, even the birds or animals that are almost hidden by the greenery. Look even closer and see the patterns in the leaves and the different shades of green. See the tiny paths through the grass and feel the animals that passed along them. Imagine what it would be like to be a small creature here.

Now look even closer and feel the spirits floating on the breeze, wrapped in the branches of a tree or hidden behind the petals of a flower. Feel your own spirit, like a shadow, behind you. Try to imagine it reaching out to join these other spirits. What would it be like to waft on the wind or float on the incoming tide? Feel yourself floating there with the other spirits. Feel the freedom and the inner calm of no cares, no worries, no needs. Just being.

If you are walking through trees imagine the spirits among them. Enjoy their company and reach out to them as you walk by.

About two miles from where I live there is a patch of wilderness I call the Parade, a natural straight clearing between two tree-crowded hummocks. It looks like a parade-ground with spectator stands on both sides. The first time I walked down there, I felt I was being watched and to my left I could indeed see dark shadows flickering among the trees. I reached the end and was wondering if I had the courage to enter the woods when one and then another young black bullocks popped out from the trees further up the hill. I had to laugh at what I'd thought were my spirit guides – but my perception that I was being observed had been right.

Once you are on your pilgrimage, watch that you don't get trapped by your own expectations. You may be 'simply wandering' but only too aware that there is a tea room at the far end of the beach, which sells particularly nice scones. It would, of course, be a very pleasant surprise if you ended up there!

Use your intuition all the time. If a stone catches your eye, stop and examine it. Try to work out what is special about it. Imagine what it would be like to be a spirit sitting there. Perhaps you feel an urge to take the stone with you or to move it to another spot. If it damages nothing and hurts no-one then why not do so? You may not understand your intuitive urge but that doesn't mean you shouldn't follow it.

It is good to bring home gifts from your pilgrimage. They can be anything that appeals to you: stones, crystals, pieces of wood, feathers. A friend of mine often returns with parts of an animal skeleton. Whatever you choose, it will be a reminder of the pilgrimage.

You will know when the pilgrimage is over because you will feel the desire to return home. Sometimes, of course, you may wish to carry on but realise that it is getting late, dusk may be falling, and you have to be sensible. There is always another day.

AFTER YOUR PILGRIMAGE

Pilgrimages are as much from something as to somewhere. You need to remember this and consider, with fresh eyes, your daily life and how it can be improved. Also, now that you are home, you need to try to understand the lessons learned and how they can be brought into your daily life.

You should write down everything in your journal that happened to you during the day. Conjure up the sense of peace and calm that you felt on the pilgrimage; re-create the sense of distance from the mundane and irritating. If you have collected any mementoes, put them in your sacred space or on your altar. Write about them in your journal, or maybe draw them.

A pilgrimage should be something to cherish, something special that you can take out and enjoy days, weeks, even years after the event. If you have a stressful job, take in one of your mementoes, maybe an attractive stone, and put it on your desk or where you work. Whenever you can, acknowledge it, the freedom and inspiration it represents. This will take seconds but it will remind you of what is precious.

To keep the idea of pilgrimage special, it is best not to do one too often and to make it fairly long for you. If you are less able-bodied, a couple of hours might be a long time, but if you are a regular hill-walker, all day may seem normal and you should consider pilgrimages of at least a couple of days.

Each pilgrimage should be unique. It is a mistake to try to re-create a successful one as it is never the same the second time. It would be better to add the route you found to others you take for normal walks than to do it again.

Celtic pilgrimages are different from others because they go to nowhere in particular. Like other pilgrimages, however, they are special. It is the undertaking of the pilgrimage that is important, not the destination. Walking the mist means understanding this important point, then enjoying the experience of being a Celtic pilgrim.

8

WORKING YOUR SACRED SITES

In Chapter Four you were introduced to the idea of using a sacred site as a tool for meditation. Now it is time to stop being a passive visitor. You can start to use the new ideas you've learned since you began to visit your site. You can use your intuition to find new sacred sites; you can begin to communicate with the spirits of the sites and learn how to work with them. You can even incorporate the ideas and emotions behind pilgrimage in the briefest of visits to your site. But, above all, you need to realise that your needs have changed since your first cautious and uncertain visit. You are unlocking your spirit and it has its own demands which are as important at your body's physical needs.

CHOOSING NEW SITES

In the beginning I started using different sites without being aware of it. Sometimes I would wander, intending to visit one site but finding myself at another; sometimes I would fight all the pointers, go where I intended, and find it was an unsatisfactory visit.

It came to a head one stormy Samhain when I was meditating at dusk on top of the Faery Hill. In my mind's eye I saw the land laid out around me in strange, shaded outlines. There was the Faery Hill and to the south of that the river valley winding easterly. Doon Hill and the ancient temple site loomed to the southeast. Far to the west was the Gathering – the first site I had ever worked. And then, suddenly, I saw a new site: the Sacred Grove.

It was like a computer game. Somehow I had moved up a level and now there was a new site to be explored. I had passed some test, acquired some skill or tool, and was being rewarded. This was happening at a time of intense pressure at work, and I had been hurried and half-hearted over the exercise. The stormy night mirrored my internal turmoil.

I pondered what to do. By now it was dark but the urge I felt to visit the site was so strong that I decided to proceed against my better judgement.

In my new plan a burn was flowing down from the Faery Hill, and although now there isn't one, I followed its approximate direction and arrived at an old dry-stone dyke overgrown with hawthorn trees and vicious blackthorn bushes. They seemed to form a solid barrier. In the dark it was almost impossible to see anything but eventually I made out that some stones were missing from the top of the dyke. Although it was covered with brambles and moss, I could see that there had been a stile at one time.

Carefully, I clambered over and found myself surrounded by barbs and thorns. Cautiously I edged forward and was surprised to discover a path under all the tree branches. Even in the dark there was a sense of where the path was and I pressed on, uncertain of what I might find.

Very quickly I became aware of a shallow burn flowing at the side of the path and then, only a few feet further down the side of the hill, the path swung back away from the stream and into a small clearing.

All around me the hawthorn trees thrashed in the gale, but in that space, there was no breath of wind. It was tranquil – even warm. I sat down and after some time, started a beautiful and serene meditation that seemed to refresh and calm me, giving me exactly what I needed at that time. It protected me, gave me peace and space to put things into perspective. That incident was responsible for my rediscovery of my spiritual path and allowed me to make the time to take major steps down it. Even today it is a site I return to whenever I feel anxious and need calming.

You can ask for help in finding new sites but it will only happen when the time is right. We are not, I believe, best equipped to know our own needs. Once different sites have been shown to you, you can choose which to visit. Initially, however, all we can do is indicate to the spirits and guides who work with us that we are keen to find new sites. They will decide if it is appropriate and whether or not we are ready.

Visualisation to Find a New Sacred Site

First, undertake the Meditation Exercise. When you are filled with white light for the third time, hold it in your body and seek to clear your mind.

Now ask, 'Great Spirits who work with me, I thank you for all your help and guidance. Help me now. As I walk this land, can you show me where to go?' Repeat this question and imagine the words swirling slowly around you as you say them, see them floating on the air.

Now imagine your body dissolving until all that is left of you is an oval of white light. Now you are this pure white light. You are aware that a warm breeze is blowing, so softly you hardly know it's there. Slowly you feel yourself moving over the landscape around you. It feels good and you are contented to float on the wind. As you move you are aware of where you are coming from and now, as you look ahead, of where you are going to. The site is now in view and you feel keen to be there.

Now you are there. You look around and know this place. It is beautiful and peaceful. It is welcoming. You thank the site for calling to you. Pause now and enjoy the simple sensation of being there. Take as long as you like.

Now you must return to your body. Let go of the new site and drift peacefully back to where you started. Slowly, slowly.

Become aware again of your body. Feel the body closing around you. You are home. Make your sign for ending spiritual work. When you are ready open your eyes.

If you find that when you try this exercise you are not called anywhere, it means that this is not the time for you to move on.

It is no reflection on you and happens to all of us. Once you know a few sites, you will find you are called to one you have already visited.

PREPARING TO VISIT A SITE

You will soon realise that different sites exert a different pull on you at different times. At any given point in your life some sites will be stronger and more special than others. I have some sites that I visit almost daily and little preparation is possible. Other sites, however, are either much further away or, like the sacred grove, sites that I feel the need to visit only occasionally. Then I need to prepare carefully, although in a perfect world the steps I describe below should apply to any visit.

Decide in advance that you are going to undertake a visit. This means that no matter when during the day you leave to visit the site you will have been aware of it at least for several hours and perhaps for a few days. This is important: it allows your subconscious to prepare itself and, if you know the site well, may even send some awareness to it.

Next, consider why you want to visit the site. If you feel a calling but are uncertain why, you can try meditation, perhaps in front of your shrine, and seek guidance on why you should go there. Once in the meditative state, ask your domestic spirits for inspiration: 'Help me, Spirit of the House [insert name if you have one], I feel a calling. Help me to know the question to ask, the answer to seek and the understanding to act.' You should return to your shrine after the visit to thank the spirits for their help and to reveal to them what happened.

Often, of course, the idea just pops into your head, and that is fine: there is no need to attempt to find grand revelations every time you visit a site. To go there and enjoy the fresh air, the exercise, the open space is often a cure in itself. The important point is not to ignore the urge.

After a ritual cleansing (see page 41), it will be time to set out for the site. It is best to do this on your own or with your dog – even though it may sometimes distract you. Do not take your mobile phone or any other electrical device. If you feel you must take the phone, switch it off and bury it in your bag so you are not tempted to use it or check for messages.

To enter into the spirit of the day and to work with the nature around you it is best to walk from your home to the site. If that is not possible, drive to around a mile from the site, or as far away as you can walk comfortably.

If you are walking all the way, the closing of the house door is the opening of your visit. If you are driving, once you have parked the car, create an opening gesture you are comfortable with, like bowing towards the site or raising your palms to the sky.

You are now on your way. No matter how hard you try, your mind will wander as different ideas are triggered by what's going on around you. And that is fine. For example, you might suddenly think that it would be nice to have a piece of ash wood and then you realise you are beside an ash tree and, of course, a small wand is lying on the ground. Or you might remember an errand you had intended to do. If it is not something you can deal with at that moment, like a phone call, write it down and forget about it.

Sometimes you will feel you have found an answer to the purpose of the visit even before you reach the site. Carry on regardless: any understanding needs to be within the whole context of the visit to the site and you don't know what will happen next.

How you approach the site is also important. If it is a well-known one – a ring of stones or an ancient holy well – then traditionally sacred paths would lead to it. If you can find them, that is a bonus. There may be local traditions about what to wear and what to do when you are there. For example, visitors to St Kevin's Well near the Glendasan river at Glendalough in central Ireland still tie small strips of material to a nearby birch tree so that a little of themselves lingers there long after they have left. Months later you can imagine your ribbon on that tree in that place of serene magic. This tradition stretches back probably to Druidic times and is, of course, replicated throughout the Celtic lands.

USING YOUR INTUITION AT THE SITE

We have already speculated on the sources of your intuition and, of course, it may be internal or external. The important point is that your conscious mind does not dictate what you think and do. In terms of visiting and working the site, if it feels good do it.

There are several points to look out for. Be aware of possible signs as you prepare for and walk to the site – for example, branches across the track or animals that do not behave as normal. Try to understand what the signs are saying to you. If you do not feel comfortable, turn back.

This happened to me one day. I walk the same way along the river with my dog. After a while the path forks: to the right it leads to a group of silver birches, a site I often visit; to the left it continues along the river. Further down the valley the paths rejoin. My old terrier was a great companion and I learned to follow her at this point. To this day I have no idea why she chose which way to go. But if you do this, be careful: my young dog would just lead you to the local hotel bins, given half a chance!

If you suddenly notice an unusual tree, rock formation or plant, stop and examine it. Try to work out why you noticed it. Sometimes it just enhances your enjoyment, a sign that you are on the right path. If you have always followed a particular route or carried out the same practices and have the urge to change it, do so.

Often we cannot understand the significance of an event. But we need to be open to the flows of nature and simply follow them. It may be that the change has nothing to do with us. Don't start look for runaway trucks that would have mown you down if you'd walked where you always walk: it's probably something much more subtle than that. Though you never know!

WORKING WITH THE SPIRITS OF THE SITE

So far we have considered sites only as places where you can experience energies to help you meditate and receive inspiration. However, the energy that attracts us also attracts other spiritual beings. Communion with them is not easy and may be confusing. It can also be rewarding as they may inspire, inform, teach and make us more aware of the spiritual world around us, thus keeping in perspective the materialistic side of life.

Like us, however, the spirits are not all of one mind. While they are not malevolent, it is easy for us to misunderstand them or, indeed, for them to misunderstand us. Several times I have found myself face to face with one of the spirits of a site and unable to understand what they want or make them understand what I want. This may seem strange to you as you read this but in time you will come to understand.

The first stage in seeking to interact with the spirits of a site is to make an offering to them and to the site. Remember that whatever you give will be of no value to the spirit: they cannot drink wine or eat cake. But the offering must be of value to you, if not in a monetary sense; leaving a Gucci handbag at the site will only confuse an already unclear situation. Rather, it has to be something of some other value to you. The spirits will respond to the act of giving and appreciate it.

To decide what to leave, try the following meditation.

Meditation to Find Your Clan Totem

Begin with the usual Meditation Exercise. After you have filled your body with white light for the third time, stop and simply be aware. Let your mind wander. Thoughts will come in and flow out. Go with them. Gradually you will feel your mind clear. Now you are in a black space. It is warm and comfortable but dark. You can see nothing in front of you. Look to your left, still nothing. Look to your right, all is dark.

Now turn and you can see an old green wooden door.

Weathered planks are held together with thick black metal brackets. There is a large round metal handle but when you pull on it nothing happens.

Now you also see that there is big old-fashioned key in the lock. It turns easily and the door swings gently open away from you. You can see green pasture stretching away and sloping gently downwards. Away in the distance softly rounded hills are shrouded in a thin mist, which turns their dark greens and light browns into faint whispers of colour.

There is a path leading across this meadow and you follow it, enjoying the view and feeling at home. Birds are singing and you feel a desire to stay and enjoy the moment. It would be lovely to sit down on the short grass and feel the balmy wind blow across your skin.

Then you remember that you have a purpose. You are here to discover your gift. The gift that you will take to the sacred site. Now you are walking more purposefully forward. That's right! You have to discover what your gift to the site will be. You know you will find it.

You reach an old wooden fence with a stile over it. You climb over, and as you do so you notice a small grove of trees off to your left. There is no path now but the grass is short and it is easy to walk. You head for the trees, almost bouncing over the mounds of grass. Now you are at the edge of the wood and it is cooler, but pleasant under the wide-spreading branches. There are not many trees here and you can see through them to a clearing and blue sky above. A very old tree is standing in the middle of the clearing. Its branches are long and strong but it has no leaves. It is not dead, though: you know this.

Strangely, you now realise you can't see it clearly. You thought you could but, no, something is hanging from its branches. Something you can't quite make out. You are getting excited. You know that whatever is hanging there is the gift you need to take to the sacred site. It is your clan totem. This you know. And you are keen to discover what it is. What better *gift to offer than the symbol of your family, its secret emblem?*

Now you are at the edge of the clearing, looking across at this tree, but you still cannot make out what it is. You start to walk across the clearing and now you are standing under the tree. You look up and there it is: your clan totem. There are several: pick one and thank the tree for this gift. Place it at the foot of the trunk as a gift of thanks and love. Look again at the old tree and see how beautiful it is, covered with your clan totem. You smile to yourself. You are happy.

Now close your eyes and become aware again of your body. Feel the sensations in your arms and legs. Feel purifying white light flow through your body from your head into your chest, through your legs and into the ground. Feel your body whole and complete. Close down, using your gesture, and open your eyes.

This meditation was first devised by Caitlin and John Matthews in a different form. They argue that the clan totem is a symbol shared with those who have walked the path before. Perhaps it is better viewed as a key. I have found, however, that it is something personal to you and therefore an ideal gift to give to the spirits of the sacred site. Because of its potential symbolic power, it is best not to tell anyone what it is.

If you find that it is not possible to make a gift of, say, a beech tree every time you visit your sacred site, find something that is linked with your totem. You will be amazed how empowering and spiritual it is to offer a gift to the spirits. Indeed, you will find that after a couple of times, when you approach the site a greater welcome awaits you.

The next stage is to talk to the spirits, tell them about yourself, your hopes and ambitions. If you do this after meditation, when you are calm and receptive, you will eventually become aware that they are listening, that they are with you. I suppose I'm saying that you need to build a relationship with the spirits. When you are comfortable with them and they with you, you can move on to deepen that relationship.

The more you visit the site, the more you will learn about it and the spirits who are there. It is as if you are learning how to 'tune in' to it. Do not be scared to explore ideas and visions that come to you: they will become increasingly powerful. You can learn a lot about yourself and your spiritual maturity by the way you react to them.

At the old temple site at Doon Hill, the small hut that was the Druids' main temple is marked out in concrete lines. Once when I was meditating there I 'saw' the hut materialise around me. The vision was so powerful that I could feel the fetid heat, smell the stale straw and raw incense, and even see the men. Suddenly one of the wizened leaders turned and looked straight at me. He started to shout and gestured for me to leave. I was so shocked he could see me that I did nothing. Then he was pushing me away with his own hands. When I opened my eyes and looked about I had been moved back about ten feet.

That frightened me. I really felt that I had reached back perhaps 1500 years. I started meditating outside the hut. Occasionally the powerful image of the village would return but I was ignored and I never tried to enter the hut.

A couple of years later when I was at the temple, I simply forgot and returned to my normal site. Again the old man was there and again he turned against me. This time, perhaps because I had grown so much more confident, I resisted him and instead transformed myself into a young but sturdy tree – an oak, I think. The old man fell back and the scene faded. I have not seen him since. But the important thing for me was that I was learning to take control of situations. It is too easy to be the victim, but that gets us nowhere. I felt great: empowered and emboldened by the experience.

At this stage you should not seek to summon spirits. First, there is no need: my experience is that the spirits are more than keen to make contact with you. Second, to summon someone is not the way of friendship and should be resisted. If you find that there is no ambience at the site, that it feels empty and lacking in energy, do not despair: return to your first site and try again. Perhaps you misunderstood the images and messages that were given to you.

HEARING THE MUSIC OF THE GODHEAD

We can visit these sacred sites on different levels. To begin with a site is somewhere we like to be, where we can practise some meditation and feel better for it. There is a deeper level at which we can become aware of the spirits of the site, feel their presence and commune with them. They can help us find answers to questions about our life and also show the irrelevance of so much in the 'real world' that is important to many. They are living proof that there is a spiritual dimension to our world and our lives.

There is however another, even deeper level. It is fun and rewarding to work with the spirits but, like them, we are seeking. There is another reason why we are drawn to these sites.

For a long time I wondered why they were so important. Again and again I was led back to the sites or shown new ones. It took me a long time to work out what was happening because so many exciting and challenging things can happen at a site. But all these events, images, spirits, historical episodes, hint at a greater experience, and that is hearing the Music of the Godhead.

The Divine Spark is within us all. Most creatures are too busy surviving to give it any thought. Even humans rarely think of spiritual things. Those who do are aware that we are still far away from the Godhead: the eternal centre from which we all come and to which we will all eventually return. Hearing the music is to catch sight of an image of return. Being at a site is like switching on a radio: at first all you hear is static, then you pick up snatches of talk, but not the station you're looking for. Sometimes the programme snippets are so interesting that you stop and listen, perhaps even forgetting why you switched on the radio.

Eventually, if you are lucky and determined, you find the station and then you have to search for a pure signal. To find that pure signal is to find the music of the Godhead. To hear the music is to know that you are on the right track; that the work you are doing is helping you, bringing you closer in some way to the Godhead, and that you need to persevere and have patience to succeed.

Christians talk of the voice of God and how they feel when they hear it. I call this experience music because, to me, words are not enough to convey the feeling. I once heard a description of what it was like to be inside the great Neolithic burial mound at Newgrange by the river Boyne in Ireland on the winter solstice as the sun rises over the hills and a concentrated beam of golden white light creeps up the stone tunnel to burst into the central chamber. That description of excitement, euphoria, awe and grateful appreciation can explain only a little of what I felt when I heard the music of the Godhead. I told a group that it was so fabulous a sensation that I would crawl over broken glass to experience it again. It is the very joy of life itself.

It explains why the Coptic fathers retreated to the desert, why the Druids forsook family life, and why the Celtic monks welcomed abstinence and the bleak lives they endured.

Today, however, we must be more pragmatic. I suspect many of the ancient monks were probably energy junkies, moving from site to site seeking new and greater 'highs'. Always remember that no matter how strong the urge, you must return to the material world. At least in this lifetime.

Part Two

DEVELOPING YOUR SKILLS

9

CREATING AND USING RITUALS

Alexander Carmichael travelled around the Highlands of Scotland in the late part of the nineteenth century and discovered a people who still followed many of the traditions and rituals of their ancestors. This was a world that has all but disappeared now, so we must be grateful for his work and that of others like him.

Dr Carmichael found a community in which the people lived so close to the spiritual world that it influenced their every thought, action and decision. In this world, people relied on rituals and prayers to protect them and to appease the elemental gods. Although they were Christian, many of their rituals and blessings were clearly pagan in origin and may have dated back to pre-Christian times.

A ritual can be something we do from habit. We often talk about our 'nightly ritual' and by that we mean the things we do just before going to bed. In this chapter we are interested in another kind of ritual: actions that we perform to link our experiences of the spiritual world more closely with our daily life. We've already talked about bringing Angel Cards to the workplace. This chapter suggests ways to take this idea further. Remember, to the Celt there was no distinction between the spiritual and material worlds, something we find difficult to understand. Ritual helps us bridge that gap.

To begin with, follow the rituals outlined in this chapter as closely as you can, but later, as you grow in confidence and you feel you understand some of the subtleties of what we are trying to achieve, feel free to vary and change them. Then think of other situations in your life to which you would like to introduce that great sense of spiritual presence. There is no limit to what you

can do, where you can do it and how it can be done. *You* are
the only limit.

CREATING RITUALS IN YOUR EVERYDAY LIFE

Many of us already have rituals in our lives, but we don't recognise them as such: for example, getting up in the morning and
having a quiet cup of tea before the day starts. The word 'ritual'
conjures up images of candles and complicated ceremonies, but
it can be as simple as taking the time to make a drink and enjoy
that procedure for what it is.

For a ritual to work, we must be conscious of what we are
doing. Many actions that could be seen as a ritual simply become
a habit – tea-drinking in the morning, for instance: perhaps the
first time you really enjoyed the tea, sat and thought pleasantly
of the day ahead and of all the nice things that might happen.
The next morning, remembering how much you enjoyed it the
day before, you did it again. This time you were a bit preoccupied and so drank the tea, almost without thinking, while
you worried about your problems. After a few days you are making the tea with only the vaguest memory of having enjoyed it;
now it is simply something you do.

The first step in creating a ritual is to decide on an opening
action. This serves several purposes. First, it is a sign to yourself
that you are about to do something significant, something that
relates to your spiritual practice. This activates the non-practical
part of the brain. The action should be different from your
symbol for spiritual practice because, although they are related,
ritual is much more wedded to the material world. You could
bow like Buddhist monks do, or clasp your hands together as if
in prayer. You could write a symbol in the air in front of you or
move a ring from one finger to another. The choice is yours. I light
a candle, or imagine lighting one if the situation isn't appropriate. So, in the morning I make a cup of tea and sit with a lit
candle; I think a little about the candle and what it signifies as

well as planning the day ahead. This prompts me to include several spiritual events. If I'm going shopping, for example, I may plan to stop in the park for a short while.

Here now are four situations into which you can easily introduce rituals. I follow them all and have found them helpful.

Start of the Day

Take some time to think of spiritual matters. They don't have to relate exactly to your practise but you might sit in your sacred space and read a couple of pages of an inspirational book. You could take time to do some work on your journal, or reread what happened the day before and enjoy the experiences all over again. To mark this moment in the day, light a candle or, if that is not possible, hold a crystal or other favourite talisman. The aim is to make a gesture to show yourself that you are doing something special and not just sitting.

At Work

If it is possible, create a sacred space at work. If you haven't much room or personal items are frowned on, take a photo of your sacred space at home, put in on the back of your locker door or in a drawer where you will often see it. Think about your working day and regular events that happen within it and how you could introduce an inspiring ritual to them. At coffee-break time, you could recite a short verse that inspires you, or water and tend any plants.

Generally we are different people at work; we have different friends, talk about different things (mostly work related) and even behave differently; the harassed young mother of three becomes the highly competent secretary of the company boss. One way of trying to integrate these two spheres is to take photos of your family in to work. As you work, you will be aware of the photos, which will bring your family to you. The problem with this is that soon you no longer notice them. So, a ritual might be that each morning you take the photos out of a drawer and place them on your desk, or place of work and each night you put them away again. Nothing fancy, but effective. In the morning you will remember your family as you left them and at night you can anticipate meeting them again and perhaps even think of funny stories from work that day to tell them.

At Home

There are endless possibilities for introducing ritual into the home. Just one example illustrates this. Think about housework: cleaning, tidying, vacuuming, ironing, washing. These are all mundane tasks. One way to introduce ritual here is to stop every time you pass your altar or sacred space and make some sign of acknowledgement. You might bow or touch something on the altar, repeat a mantra or a phrase. For a moment, you are taken out of your housework stupor and into your spiritual dimensions. You might find it activates thoughts and ideas of a more spiritual kind while you work.

Travelling

When we are in cars, planes, buses and trains, we are detached from the land and alienated from its energies. Try to find ways to overcome this. I am reminded of a holiday I had in Malta where the buses and taxis all had shrines to the Virgin Mary at the front. Before they set out, taxi drivers would say a little prayer. It didn't inspire confidence in me, but I liked the idea of constantly being in touch with the spirits. Why not place some items in your car? We have a piece of ash wood, a twig we found that had broken off the tree. Ash is a good wood to have in the car as one of its properties is to protect travellers.

In public transport, as you sit and look out of the window, try the following visualisation.

Travelling Visualisation

Make yourself comfortable and when you are ready make the sign for starting spiritual work. If it feels appropriate close your eyes, and then, using the Sitting Simply exercise, try to achieve inner peace.

Now imagine that you are filled with fizzing white energy. See it like a great column four or five feet high coming out of the top of your head and falling back slightly as you speed along. Like a great sherbet fountain, imagine it cascading out, sparkling in the light and falling on to the land as you travel. Imagine that every sparkle is a blessing and see this trail of glittering energy as you pass by. Do this for as long as you feel you can and then stop. Make your sign to finish spiritual work.

As you sit, or doze, while travelling along, repeat this visualisation several times. If you feel tired or drained, stop. But it's quite fun and normally I find it buoys me up.

RITUALS FOR SPIRITUAL PRACTICE

We are already using many rituals in our practice – such as the opening and closing gestures for spiritual work. Rituals can enhance our spiritual practice as they enrich our experiences by acknowledging our own discoveries and also those of others. They also allow us to weave sometimes quite complex ideas and values into our actions.

For example, you should always take particular note of things you do that seem to work well for you and then try to make them a regular part of your practice. You might find that you run out of white candles and have to use blue while you are Sitting Simply. Perhaps with the blue candles you feel calmer and more serene. Why not use blue candles when you want to conjure up that sense of well-being? Try to understand why this has happened. In this example blue is the colour of spiritual development.

It may be that before you meditate at your site, you like to walk round it a couple of times. Why not? Make it part of your ritual. Often you will find later that rituals you have devised are similar to those of others. At first when this happened to me I was taken aback; now I find it reassures me.

In Part One I outlined many different ways for you to undertake spiritual work. In every case rituals can enhance the experience for you.

Opening Gestures for Spiritual Work

Consider the gesture that you currently use and why you chose it. Perhaps it was suggested to you and you felt comfortable with it. Perhaps it was an idea that just popped into your head and seemed right. If you bow to the east before you start, why did you choose to face east? In fact, it is a traditional position. Celtic churches faced east so that as the sun rose the rays would fall on to the altar. The dead were often buried with their feet towards the east so that they faced the rising sun. Why do you bow? It is a good action because it is non-rational: you are bowing apparently to no one. In truth you may feel that you are paying respect to a being. In ancient times, to bow was a symbol of trust in the person to whom you bowed – your eyes had to look away as your body bent so you were trusting them not to attack you.

Consider what you want to achieve with your opening gestures: you wish to indicate to yourself and the spirits that surround you that you are about to begin spiritual work. Implicit in this is a request for their help, co-operation and a token of respect. You should consider whether you wish to indicate anything else in your opening gestures, such as humility or trust, then try to think of rituals that would indicate this.

You also need to decide whether it would be suitable to have different gestures in different situations. This is where ritual comes in: it saves you having constantly to reinvent the wheel. Take some time now to consider what your opening ritual should include, devise it and write it down in your journal.

My core gesture is a bow to the east with arms folded. This is part of all my opening and closing ceremonies. However, when I am in the house, I include the lighting of candles to create a focal point for me. This reminds me of when I was a child and an elderly aunt of my mother would look into the fire with me, show me dead relatives and tell me stories about them. For me candles conjure images of safety and being loved, as well as an element of psychic activity. All of this, of course, is highly conducive to spiritual work.

Rituals for Meditation

Can you think of anything that would enhance your meditation? After your opening gestures, is there anything else you would like to do either before or during your meditation? For example, perhaps you find it difficult to keep your eyes closed. Perhaps, if you are outside, you feel as if people are watching or approaching you. If that is so you might want to create a ritual to help you keep your eyes closed. To do this you could add a gesture as you settle down. Once you are ready to meditate, keep your eyes open. Spend a couple of minutes simply looking about you to take in the landscape. Now close your eyes and gently place a finger on each eyelid, hold them there for a minute, then let go. Open your eyes and look around you again: see how everything has remained the same. When you are ready, close your eyes and this time start the Meditation Exercise (see page 33).

When you are floating, try this ritual: keep your eyes closed but refocus as if you were trying to see the bridge of your nose. Feel the tightness in your eyes, then relax. Repeat this twice. Now, still with your eyes shut, deliberately let your eyes slip out of focus. It feels as if your eyes are moving further apart and it will seem as if you are looking into a great cavern of red-brown stone. You will feel as if you are being surrounded, as if you were entering this cave. Accept this sensation, stop and enjoy it. Now continue with the rest of your exercise. The focus on your inner sight distracts you from other worries or concerns, gives you a sense of safety and justifies why your eyes have to be closed.

By sitting and thinking about how, where and when you meditate, what you like and don't like about your exercises, you can devise rituals to help overcome the problems and enhance the enjoyment.

Rituals at Sacred Sites

People react differently to the energies and spirits at a sacred site. Spend some time considering if you feel that there are actions you should be undertaking but have so far failed to do. For example, at your site there may be specific entities, gods and goddesses, that you have failed to acknowledge. Only a few sacred sites still have such presences but it is possible that they are there. If it feels right to you, you may wish to introduce a ritual into your practices to pay homage to them.

To find out if there is a god or goddess at your site, try the following exercise. If you are nervous about the idea of communing with ancient gods and goddesses, this exercise is perfect for you because you do it at home away from the site and never need come into contact with the entities, if they are there. If a saint is associated with your site, this exercise will help you find out if he or she is still there.

Searching for Gods and Goddesses

At night, as you are going to sleep, try the following visualisation. Make the gesture to start spiritual work. Imagine that you are standing at your sacred site. Look about you and notice all the sights you are familiar with. Feel the calm security of being somewhere you know and feel safe.

Now look down and see that there is a wide black hole in the ground. The top of a wooden ladder is sticking out of it and glowing white lights show a wide well stretching deep down into the ground.

Grasp the top of the ladder and begin to climb down. Quickly you reach the bottom and when you look up you can see the clear blue sky far above you. You are at your sacred site, and safe. You look around and see a short corridor leading to a wooden door.

It is ajar so push it. The door opens to reveal a cavern with a curtain the far end. Look around you. What do you see?

If the cave is empty, there are no gods or goddesses at your site. If there is some old furniture, broken and covered with cobwebs and dust, then there were Gods or Goddesses at your site but no longer.

If the cavern is well furnished, with a roaring fire and food on the table, gods or goddesses are present. Now you can leave and climb back up the ladder. When you reach the ground, breathe in the sweet fresh air. Make the sign to close spiritual work, then begin to return to where you are lying in bed.

Using Ritual on Pilgrimage

As you walk over the moors or along the sides of lochs, as the wind ruffles your hair and the lofty mountains tower over you, your pilgrimage comes alive. It is almost impossible to imagine in advance what your emotions will be once you are out of your daily confines and free on the trail, so it is difficult to stick to any set plan.

Rituals can help you open up to the true potential of a Celtic pilgrimage. Take some paper and a pen with you. When you stop, as suggested, after a minute to look about and to root yourself in the land, why not also write down your hopes for the pilgrimage? It may be that you want to explore why you felt such anger with your partner for some silly thing they said; or perhaps you have been offered a new job and want to know whether to accept it.

After you have written it down, bury the piece of paper, either literally in the ground or under a stone or a pile of leaves. Connect it with the earth and, as you do this, repeat, 'May the spirits and angels of this site help me find the answer I seek.' Once you have done that, stand up and feel the anxiety over that issue as a hard ball at the back of your neck. Now feel it melt through your body and down on to the ground. See it, with your mind's eye, flow over to where the paper is and dissipate. Feel the relief. As you begin to walk, your steps are lighter. Stop and reconnect with your surroundings. Smile. Thank the angels and spirits of the site and move on, forgetting about your problem. As you undertake your pilgrimage, don't think about it. If it comes into your mind, remember that if it is there, it can't be with the spirits, and hasten to banish it. You will get an answer but it may well be after the pilgrimage is over. That is normal.

Creating Sacred Ceremonies

Ceremonies, unlike rituals, are often tied, not to spiritual practise, but to helping us mark changes in our lives. Stag nights and weddings are examples of this.

Ceremonies can also be used to mark transitions in the world around us. For the Celts the most significant ceremonies marked the changing of the seasons, but here we are interested in the personal.

If you feel uncomfortable about involving other people in your spiritual work, don't worry. Spiritual development is a personal thing, and ideas and practices that you find acceptable, others may find odd, uncomfortable or even threatening.

Ceremonies may have a private part and a public part. Birthdays should always be marked because it is the completion of a year, a turn of the sun, a celebration of being alive. The private part of the birthday may be an exchange of gifts with your partner and family. Perhaps a public ceremony, a lunch party with some friends, will follow.

You can create ceremonies for anything you like: buying a new house, a child's first day at school or the start of your holidays. When something bad happens, a ceremony may be a way of acknowledging the pain, coping with it and leaving it behind. Depending on the issue, this may take some time and involve more than one ceremony.

Death is one of those issues that are difficult for us in our sanitised Western world. Many of us pass most of our lives without seeing a dead body, let alone dealing with the grief and loss that death can bring. This is an area where a combination of conventional and private ceremonies can help you.

When my Gran was dying, she had been seriously ill for a while and we had all agreed her passing on would be a blessing. None the less when it happened, I was surprised that I was very upset. She had always been there for me and, when I was younger, I had felt really close to her.

The last night, as she lay in hospital, I was at home, restless and vaguely distressed. Eventually I felt the calling of the land, and slipped out into the dark countryside. I walked down the lane, trying to remember all the good times with her, the simple times that you take for granted: having Sunday tea, going shopping in Glasgow, waiting for her to get off the bus. Times you can't imagine ending when you are young.

I reached a spot we call the Faery Dell because faeries have been sighted there. I called out to them spontaneously and asked them, if they could, to ease her transition into the next world. As I did this, I thought of how unlikely it was that they could do anything and yet how right it had felt to make the request. I looked up and, as I did, a shooting star raced up across the sky like a soul soaring to heaven. And as that star soared so did my emotions, a great wave of grief crashed over me and I burst into tears. It took me several minutes to regain my composure. I remember feeling shocked at its suddenness and violence, and yet also in that moment there was a great beauty and calm. I said goodbye to her in that moment, and was happy to do so. As a ceremony it was simple and private, though it was something I could later share with others.

My Gran actually died a few hours later and I took the news calmly. A few days later, her funeral was the public part of my farewell ceremony. It was sad but clinical. There was no sense of her being there, she was gone, with all our love, to the next stage of her journey. But still the public funeral helped me: it was a sign of completion. We could all now move on.

Ceremonies do not need to be kept for the dramatic times in our lives. Whenever there is a moving on or a transition, a ceremony, large or small, is appropriate. In the nature of our work, my partner and I travel a lot: when we leave a hotel room we always take a moment to thank it for its shelter and comfort. It's nice to spend a few minutes in a busy day just acknowledging the moving on.

Sit down and think of any transitions coming up in your life: children leaving home, a holiday, a birthday, retirement. Then think of how you would like to mark that transition. If you want, the public part of the ceremony might be a party or a get-together with friends. Some of the people there may know why you arranged it but you don't need to tell everyone.

The private part of the ceremony should involve part of what you want to leave behind and part of what you want to take with you. For example, if you are moving house, you may want to leave a gift for the people moving in and take some cuttings from your favourite plants to remind you of good times you've had.

Changing Rituals

The Celts were great traditionalists and it is likely that the rituals they observed were hundreds of years old and unchangeable. Today we can be pragmatic about these things. Once you have created or copied a ritual you should recognise that it meets a need so you should continue with it.

However, we should be aware that times and our needs change: it may not be appropriate to carry on with rituals that worked for us ten years previously. There is a danger that obsessive compulsive behaviour may creep in, and I tend to fall into this trap all too often. The fear arises that if you leave out part of a ritual it won't work. Intellectually I know this not to be true but the adage 'Better safe than sorry' springs all to readily to my mind.

With my writing, for example, I have to meditate, light candles and prepare myself before I start. On one occasion I was staying in a hotel room where no naked flames were allowed and I panicked, believing that if I couldn't light candles, I couldn't write. Rituals are there to help us, not to set up blocks or hinder us. It is useful to check yourself every now and then and ask why you are still doing a certain ritual and if it really still works for you. After all, if you change it, it might work even better.

10

WORKING WITH THE RHYTHMS OF NATURE

We live in strange times. More and more people crave to live in our towns and cities yet long for a rural idyll. And, of course, while many people love walking among trees, or along the shore of a deserted beach, few have any desire to stroll through a cement works or industrial estate. That is not to say that cities do not have their attractions, with clubs, restaurants, shops, cinemas, galleries and museums. Only a fool would deny it, and many councils are striving to introduce greenery into the bleakest pile of bricks and concrete.

For the Celt the idea of living in a city would have been alien. Until around AD 900 there were no large settlements in either Scotland or Ireland. Celts lived in small family-based *clachans* that came together under a local king for greater protection. It should be of no surprise, then, that the religion of people who lived all their lives in the countryside was based in the fields and woods rather than in bleak and enclosed stone buildings. For the Celt, cities would feel like soulless places where people ignore each other, while the noise and busy importance of people, machines and enterprises, crowd out the simple, loving heartbeat of the land.

Celts worshipped in the open air. In a large version of your Sacred Space they communed with the elements. The trees were their cathedrals and the boulders their altars. The wind would blow, the water flow, and the sun shine down as they stood barefoot on the living earth.

Druids and then Celtic monks led them in services that were open to all – human and non-human. The lives of the Celtic saints are full of stories about animals being attracted to services conducted by saints like St Columba in the forests of Vosges. The holy men also worked with the elements, calming storms, summoning winds or, as with St Ninian, defying the rain. One tale of St Ninian tells of him and a companion remaining dry while they sat beside a road chanting during a downpour. Until, that is, St Ninian's attention wandered for a moment and then the rain crashed down, revealing his weakness.

The Celts welcomed the weather in all its variations. In the cycle of the year each type has a role to play. A winter without hard frost means viruses and bugs will not be killed off; a spring without rain bodes ill for the harvest in the autumn; a summer that is too hot will put woods and fields at the threat of fire and cause fish to lie deeper in the water; an autumn without wind and rain will make ploughing harder.

In our modern world farmers have machinery and chemicals to maximise output, but for the rest of us, the changing seasons should be celebrated as they mark steps on our journey through life. Each has much to offer us both physically and spiritually. By connecting more strongly with nature, your life will be nurtured and you will benefit to an unimaginable extent as you focus more on the real world, rather than the artificial one that humankind constructs.

NOTICING NATURE

It should be so easy to notice nature. How difficult can it be to look out of the window of your home each day? In fact, it is very difficult. Consider this: do you know in which phase the moon is today? Or which common tree, willow or hawthorn, flowers first?

There are many ways to reconnect with nature. Walking in the countryside or in city parks will help. If you have a garden or even just plants in the house, you can begin the process. In the garden, touch your plants, get your hands dirty with the soil. Feel the richness of the loam. Spend time with the plants and trees and, like a child, explore the hidden tracks and ways of your garden. Look under the leaves, behind the plants, between the rocks. Watch how the plants change with the seasons. Celebrate when they flower, tend them as they fall back to rest for the winter. Nurture them over the long dark period and be thrilled when the first green shoots reappear in the spring.

Get to know your patch of Gaia, and as you do so be aware of the spirits that surround everything. Sense them flowing about you as you walk in your garden. See if you can feel where they congregate and try to understand why. Use that information to create several sacred spaces in the garden for different times of the day or year.

You can also do this exercise in the house. Group several bushy plants together. Ivy is good for this, as are ferns. Create dark groves where leaves entwine and secret areas are created. As you water and nourish your plants, touch and talk to them. Spend some time examining the incredible designs on the leaves. As you let your fingers trace the patterns try to sense their life history. Maybe you grew them from seed, or bought them at a local shop.

Be aware, too, of a cycle. As we nourish our plants, they nourish us by taking the carbon dioxide from our breath and converting it to oxygen. Think of this as you do the Breathing Meditation (see page 31). I love the idea that as I breathe out, the plant breathes in, the plant breathes out and I breathe in. Of course it doesn't happen quite like that, but the image is inspiring and helps us appreciate the need to have plants around us.

I also place small carved faery figures in some of the plant pots so that wee faces peek out from between the leaves. Of course this is very twee but it reminds me of the spirits and the faeries that I would like to be around me. In one pot a wooden dragon roars out at me from behind a fern, his red eyes twinkling in the morning sunshine.

WORKING WITH THE CHANGING PERIODS
OF THE MOON

Our calendar is based on the earth's rotation around the sun, each rotation a year long. The Druids, we know, were great astronomers and would have understood this. Newgrange – that most regal of Neolithic mounds – is aligned with the winter solar solstice. Other mounds nearby are aligned to the summer solstice and the equinoxes, thus allowing the Druids to track the solar year.

Nonetheless many academics assume that they counted by the lunar cycle, each cycle being twenty-eight days. In the normal year, there are thirteen cycles of the moon and an extra day. An extra moon month was added every twenty years or so to correct the drift of the moon months getting a day earlier each year.

The moon is closely linked with the changing tides and, because of the constant tidal ebb and flow, with emotions. The word 'lunatic' stems from the idea that the moon can affect us emotionally, especially when it is full. The evidence for this is patchy and contradictory, though I do find it harder to fall asleep at the full moon and tend to have more vivid dreams. Many people I know who live in the countryside have similar experiences. It may be that the effects are less strong in the cities, with their street-lights.

We can use the cycle of the moon to strengthen our links with the natural world around us. From the new moon to the full moon, as the globe grows in the sky, then this is a time for new ideas and expanding existing plans. From the full moon to the end of the cycle is a time for consolidation and fruition. Try to begin anything new before the full moon.

Spying the New Moon
As the new moon approaches, sense the anticipation in the air. Whenever you see the new moon for the first time, stop whatever you are doing and welcome the new month. At the end of

the nineteenth century, Alexander Carmichael reported that the men of the Isle of Barra in the Western Isles would bow to the new moon and the women would curtsy. In Cornwall people would nod to the new moon and finger any silver coins they had in their pockets. In Edinburgh even men and women of learning would turn the rings on their fingers and make a wish. He quoted this verse from Inverness:

> If tonight, O moon, thou hast found us
> In peaceful, happy rest,
> May thy laving lustre leave us
> Seven times still more blest.

Think of what's coming up in the next month: Celtic fire festivals, significant days, the birthdays of family and friends, and anything else there is to look forward to. Now think of the things you hope to achieve. In your mind's eye, as you look at the new moon, see yourself achieving your goals. For example, you might want to take up a new hobby, painting, perhaps: in this first moment of the new moon, see yourself sitting before an easel painting a masterpiece. Hold that vision in your mind: it will be more vibrant for your glimpse of the new moon. Later think out how you will achieve the image you saw.

The first period of the moon is, then, the time to buy any equipment you might need – paint, paper, brushes, the all important easel, and plan how to learn the technique. Maybe a friend could teach you. Perhaps you could get a book from the library. Or maybe you just have to get on and do it.

The Full Moon
The three days of the full moon are a time for celebration, marked with special rituals, but it is difficult to achieve this because our culture pays no heed to the lunar cycle: make sure you have a calendar that shows the phases of the moon, allowing you to plan ahead.

It is curious that we seem to connect more with the moon than the sun. Often when I am away from home I will look at the full moon and think of my loved ones gazing up at it. It brings me closer to them. I never do that with the sun. I never think of them sharing its heat or its colours. It just doesn't have the same romantic appeal.

Such an attachment to the moon has brought together groups of people all over the world. In many parts of the country there are now groups who meet and go out to sacred sites to chant and drum under the brilliant white light. Here is a simpler but powerful exercise for you.

Walk to the Moon

This must be planned in advance. Choose one of the three nights of the full moon and prepare to go out for a walk in the dark when it is high in the sky. Before you go, sit in your sacred space and make the sign to start spiritual work. If you can, sit in the dark and let in the moonlight.

Do the Meditation Exercise and as you float in the blackness see the moon rise slowly and feel it illuminate and fill you with well-being and a greater sense of the invisible worlds that surround us. Let the white light work on you, feel it cleanse and fulfil you. When you are ready, turn away from it and allow everything to go dark around you, but while you are doing this, sense the presence of the moon, like a doting parent watching over you to make sure that all is well.

Now close the meditation and make the sign for closing the spiritual practice. Take a couple of minutes to gather yourself while keeping that sense of calm and peace. Remember how it felt to be connected to the moon and hold that sense inside you.

Now as you step out into the night to go for your walk, seek out the moon again and feel the flush of relief and love when you see it, like a long-lost friend. As you walk, watch it as much as you can. Keep it either within sight or in your mind's eye.

The route you choose is up to you. I follow my intuition but generally walk through a nearby village and along various country lanes. The importance lies in being out in the moonlight, not in what you do while you are there. A sacred site would distract you and it would be best not to go to one unless you feel particularly drawn.

If you live in a town or city, or feel uncomfortable about going out at night, why not just sit in a sacred space in your garden and watch the moon from there? You could even sit in the dark in your house at an open window to let in the night air and moonlight. This is truly magical. Working with the moon gives you a real sense of not just working with nature but working with the magic. Cassandra Eason's *Night Magic* captures this and is well worth reading.

MARKING THE SOLAR CYCLES

There were four major sun festivals for the Celts. The most important are the winter and summer solstices when the day is at its shortest and longest respectively. The spring and autumn equinoxes when the length of day and night is equal are of secondary importance. These festivals occur on the same date every year: winter solstice, 21 December; spring equinox, 21 March; summer solstice, 21 June; autumn equinox, 21 September.

All were marked with huge bonfires, feasting and ceremonies. You can join in with your own celebrations, like others all over the world. If you haven't space for a bonfire, or the weather is bad, you can hold your ceremony indoors. If you have a working fireplace, make a ceremony of laying a fire – if you need a fire all day long, let it die down towards the evening, then build it up with due dignity.

If you do not have a fireplace, use one candle or several. Choose colours suitable for the season: white for winter, green for spring, yellow for summer and red for autumn. Set up an appropriate space, such as a window-ledge, and let the flame of the candle kindle images of bonfires and outdoor celebrations for you.

The winter solstice is traditionally thought to celebrate mid-winter, although in fact it is only the beginning of the winter period. This solstice, of course, has been transformed into Christmas: a festival that is so all-pervasive especially in the English-speaking world that it is impossible to ignore. There are lots of books on how to celebrate a Celtic Christmas but here are some suggestions.

At the solstice we hold a big party and invite all our friends and neighbours. We have a huge bonfire and allow everyone to make of it what they want. Some are content to come out and see it lit, then drift back into the house. Others join us for some small ceremonies.

We gather round the fire and, rather like a ceilidh, each person who wants to, comes forward and recites or chants, or leads some drumming. Each of us offers the others something personal to us, something to share and enjoy. An easy option is to find some poems, or even better write your own, that sum up what the solstice means to you.

While for the Celt the New Year began early in November, the solar year ends on 21 December, so this is a good time to look back and jettison all the emotional and personal debris that accumulates. Another ceremony you can do is to take a piece of paper and write on it all the things you want to achieve physically in the new year: new projects you want to start; courses you want to attend. If the solstice falls during the first part of the moon-month, why not also include emotional debris you want to get rid of or new positive attitudes you'd like to adopt.

Wait for the bonfire to die down until there are only glowing embers. Once you've made your resolutions, wrap your paper round a silver birch twig and throw it on to the fire. Watch the small purple flames lick round it. As the smoke rises, see this as a message, a pledge to your gods. Remember to write the resolutions in your journal.

My partner and I exchange a small, spiritually inspired gift on the solstice but, like almost everyone else, we leave the rest of the presents for the twenty-fifth. To exchange gifts with family and friends is a delicious thing to do at this time of the year because, of course, the worst of the winter is yet to come. Centuries ago, it would have been foolhardy and extravagant to give away any of your food. Thus, even the simplest gifts can be seen as a sign of love and affection that we might risk future hunger to give someone else a token of our esteem.

The spring equinox is a much lower-key celebration for us when we renew the resolutions we made at the winter solstice. This is a good time for putting winter behind and beginning to enjoy the spring for, although there may still be the occasional period of bad weather, the worst is past and summer is not so far away. Symbolically it is also a time to clear out the clutter accumulated through the enforced indolence of winter. This is true both physically and emotionally

The summer solstice marks the arrival of summer and we acknowledge the power of the sun at a time when, here in Scotland, it never gets really dark. Celebrate the solstice by getting up early to watch the sun rise. Here we go to the top of the nearby hill where the temple is situated. Normally I stay up all night, meditating and walking the hills.

Many people don't realise that it gets as bright as day before the sun is over the horizon so it is quite difficult, when you are out on the hill, to know exactly when it is going to appear. As I walk the hills I watch the light change from heavy dusk to pale dawn and then to a much brighter, fresher daylight. At that point I head to the temple. There, I look due east over the North Sea and wait.

This is such an exciting ceremony to do because, of course, you know the sun will rise, but a great sense of expectation builds within you. The longer you wait, the greater the anticipation. The horizon grows brighter and small clouds in the far distance glow with reddish-yellow light. Sometimes strands of gold shoot up in various places as you scan the misty line between sea and sky, trying to guess where the sun will appear.

And suddenly it does: the sun doesn't slip over the horizon, it is suddenly there. This is a time for celebration and you cannot help but smile. All is good with the world. If you go out with a group, why not take drums and other musical instruments to greet the summer sun with songs and dancing? Have a party.

At the bonfire that night, we anticipate the heat of summer and the harvest. It is a bright open fire on a warm and balmy night. Remember the winter solstice when you were all wrapped up and enclosed and think how much better it is now to be out and free.

The autumn equinox marks a time of change with the first shadows hinting at the arrival of winter as the weather turns for the worse. With the harvest in, thoughts turn past winter to the next spring as fields are ploughed and new crops planted.

Like the spring equinox, this is a lesser festival. It is a time to acknowledge change and begin to prepare for winter. We often build a smaller bonfire and this is a night for family and close friends. I've always liked this time. I love the dark. I like walking the country lanes while the wind howls around me, or standing on the Faery Hill and feeling the elements swirl around me in great rushes of energy.

Dark nights also mean we can light candles and sit listening to music or reading in the golden light. It is a time when we start having our wood fire in the house regularly. I love the ceremony of making a fire, and it is only in the autumn and winter when we really need it – it fuels our central heating and hot-water system. So the autumn equinox is not a time of regret at the passing of summer but a celebration of the arrival of a different time of year and all the pleasures that go with it.

MARKING THE FIRE FESTIVALS

As well as these four fixed festivals, the Celts also celebrated four fire festivals that more accurately mark the change of the seasons. They were not fixed to any date in the calendar and in the past the days on which the festivals were held would have been selected by the Druids, although most likely they would have fallen on the full moon closest to: 1 November, for Samhain; 1 February, for Imbolc; 1 May, for Beltaine; and 1 August, for Lammas. Samhain and Beltaine are the two most important, with Beltaine celebrations now occurring all over Scotland. Samhain has been Christianised with Hallowe'en and secularised with Guy Fawkes Night.[2] Both Imbolc and Lammas are often given other more local names, which perhaps reflects their lesser importance.

Samhain is the festival of changeover with the arrival of the new year. This was a time, the Celts believed, when the veil between the worlds was at its thinnest, when spirits and faeries could come into our world and, if we were not careful, we might stray into theirs. The bonfire then was for protection, to keep light in the land through the hours of darkness. Guising and practical jokes took place at this time. Some have argued that disguises were designed to confuse the faeries if they came looking for you, but this seems unlikely.

Because the Celts counted from dark to light, Samhain, strictly speaking, starts at midnight on 31 October and runs until dusk on 1 November. This is a powerful time for meditation and communing with the spirits, and if at all possible you should make sure you are free as far as possible on these days.

Start the thirty-first with a long meditation. Follow that with visits to some of your favourite sacred sites and preparation for the party that night. Also, make sure you take time to review the last year – think especially of anyone close to you who has died.

---

2 A British festival of fireworks and bonfires supposedly to celebrate the foiling of a plot to kill King James VI and I in 1605.

If you have anything of theirs bring it to your sacred space and spend some time holding it and thinking of them. This is a time when they will be especially close to you. Remember all the good things they gave you and all the attributes that made them so special to you.

As dusk grows near, light a candle for these distant friends and place it in the window. We have a huge altar candle that we only use for this purpose and we take time to watch the flame. Think of it as your love shining there for all the spirits that go past to see.

If you have children, encourage them to get dressed up and go out guising if it is safe for them to do so. This is something magical that you can be part of and it helps you and your community to come together. It is fun to have wee humans at your door, singing a song or telling a joke and getting apples or nuts for it. Perhaps it just reminds me of an earlier, simpler time.

Build a great bonfire that will last all night, and light it with the flame from your candle that you lit while it was still daylight; this connects your fire with the last day of the old year and the first day of the new. We have found it is not always easy to arrange a party as Samhain as it generally falls during the week: people have been at work and don't want to be out late because they have to work the next day – if you find this is a problem, hold your celebration at the nearest weekend. On the thirty-first itself just make sure your candle will last through the night, and on the first ceremonially light a fire in the house from it or, if that is not possible, have a short ceremony before you blow it out.

Around the fire carry out whatever rituals you feel comfortable with. The importance here is to keep it going until first light. Then stir it again into life. In fact, you can do this several hours later if you don't want to stay up all night. Cover the fire with ash until you are ready to reactivate it.

The next day, 1 November, is a day of recovery, but as we are now into Samhain you need to take care. I have found it best not to do any spiritual work, especially if you are tired after a late night. Rather, walk in the countryside, sit and read inspirational books, prepare natural food and take it easy.

In the late afternoon decide where you want to go to meditate during the most spiritually powerful time of the year: dusk at Samhain. For years I went to the Faery Hill and there I experienced vivid teachings on meditation and how to use it. Latterly I have headed out into the hills to wherever I have been drawn. If spirits or gods are going to appear to you, this is the time they will choose so you need to be flexible about where you go.

It was at this time of year that the Faery Queen appeared to me. I had been meditating on the hill and was on my way back down when my dog, who normally runs around, was right between my feet. I looked down at her in surprise and then saw she was gazing back up the hill. I turned and a woman was materialising in front of me. She was of average height and wearing a white gown that looked like a Roman toga. I stared at her, and as she turned towards me, I panicked and took to my heels. Seconds later I skidded to a halt, ashamed at my fear and lack of respect. I turned round, but she was gone. Although I have never seen her again or even sensed her, I live in hope that one day I can pay her the respect she is due.

Imbolc, at the beginning of February, is the first sign that winter is on the wane. Often the snowdrops are out, their bright white petals a brilliant sign that warmer times lie ahead. Yellow and purple crocuses may be in bloom. The land is stirring. So it is with we humans, after the bleak cold December and January. Imbolc, or Brigantia as it is sometimes called, has been Christianised as the feast of St Bridgid, the midwife to the Virgin Mary; in her pagan and Christian forms she is associated with the arts and being creative. Our bonfire at Imbolc tends to be one of defiance, the fierce red and orange flames leaping into the air and the roaring heat blasting out all around us. This is a time for action – or, at least, thinking about it.

Beltaine is probably the best-known Celtic festival. At the beginning of May, spring is truly all around us. The daffodils and tulips are dying back, the gorse is in full bloom, its heady coconut scent filling the air. Hawthorn is coming into flower and wild primroses pepper the hills. The nights are now lighter and offer opportunities for outdoor activities. Summer is on the way and we are content with the world.

Beltaine, via May Day celebrations and the maypole, is also linked to fertility and the world in full bloom. However, this is puzzling because children conceived on May Day will be born at Imbolc (perhaps this is the link with St Brigid as a midwife), which is not the best time to give birth: after a hard winter, women may be prone to flu and other viruses. Beltaine's link with promiscuity must stem from the freedom that comes with late spring to be able to lie outdoors with your partner in comfort.

Lammas is the festival of the harvest. Although the beginning of August is too early for most crop gatherings, the crops are ripening and the reward for hard work is near. Throughout Europe, of course, August is the holiday month with many shops and businesses closing. In Scotland July is the traditional time of holiday but the Lammas Fair was one of the most important events of the year. Cattle sales are still conducted in some areas at this time.

Our Lammas bonfire tends to be the most hurried of all the festivals we organise. Somehow it is always an afterthought. Lammas fires should be bright and the centrepoint of a great outdoor party with perhaps a barbecue, dancing and music. At the fire, think of all the work you do and the rewards you receive for it, assess whether it's worth while and consider what you really want to do with your life. These thoughts may be the start of you reassessing your life over the winter, still so far off.

LIVING IN THE SEASONS

When you are planning your year, you can, of course, overlap the cycles of the sun, the moon and the seasons, and work out the best, most natural time to undertake any particular task. We might say, for example, that a new venture should be planned during the new-moon periods of winter, initiated with a new moon in spring, moulded into shape during the summer, then set in the autumn. Come winter, you can assess how things are going and dream of changes, developments you can make in the spring.

So, for example, if you were considering setting up a business, you should start thinking and dreaming about it between the winter solstice and Imbolc, using the creativity of Imbolc to help work out your ideas. Use the new moon for inspiration and intuition to work out what you should be doing. Then, during the second period of the moon-month, you could perhaps attend courses or research ideas. By the spring you should be in a position to put your research into operation, sort out the finance, open a bank account, look for premises. By the summer you may be ready to start trading. In the autumn, it should be settling into a pattern and the rewards will be obvious. By winter you will be ready to review how well you've achieved your initial goals and how things can be improved.

With emotional issues the same cycle applies. If you are concerned about your relationship with your partner, winter is the time to think it through. In the spring you can try to address the issues you've identified, summer would see them put to rest and a new exciting phase beginning in the relationship. The autumn sees this new relationship settling down and becoming the norm. By winter you might assess again how things have gone and think of innovations for the spring.

All of this, of course, shows how out of touch our 24/7 society is with the natural rhythms: adult education classes, school and university terms all begin in the autumn when really they should start in spring.

As spiritual beings in the material world, we need to turn away from artificial lights, all-night shopping and nightshifts. We need to learn once again how to live with the rhythms of nature. As you pay more heed to the seasons and recognise the individual energies and inspirations that different times of the year generate, you will find it easier to achieve what you want to achieve. You will begin to welcome the changes in the weather and the subsequent changes they imply in you, and you will find that you want to know the phases of the moon and the times of the high tides. As you walk along the beaches during the day or the country lanes at night, tides and moons will affect what you can and cannot do. And that is good, because it is natural!

11

WORKING WITH TREES

The Celts counted from dark to light. So – as today – the day began at midnight and the year at Samhain or Hallowe'en – 1 November. There has been speculation that moon-months would have been named after trees, given the close link between the Celts and trees. In 1948 Robert Graves created a tree calendar, and other writers have produced different versions of it. Here is the one I use. It shows the tree and its key attribute. Count from new moon to new moon, from darkness to light. The first new moon to use is the one nearest 1 November.

1–28 November	silver birch:	new beginnings
29 November – 26 December	rowan:	protection
27 December – 24 January	alder:	dreaming
25 January – 21 February	willow:	tranquillity
22 February – 21 March	ash:	meditation
22 March – 18 April	hawthorn:	purity
19 April – 16 May	oak:	knowledge
17 May – 13 June	holly:	defence
14 June – 11 July	hazel:	creativity
12 July – 8 August	vine:	prophecy
9 August – 5 September	ivy:	inner journey
6 September – 3 October	reed:	direct action
4–31 October	elder:	connections

Take some time to consider this calendar. Depending on where you live, you may want to change some of the trees. Ideally they should appear when they are at their most active or distinctive. Where that is not the case, with silver birch, for instance, other factors have been deemed more important – in this case that it stands for a fresh start.

Keep a symbol of the tree of that lunar cycle on your altar. During the month seek out trees of that species and hold small rituals round them. Perhaps you could choose a tree in your area and each year honour it during its month. You will find that the trees will respond to this and, as you perform the ceremony, you will notice a sense of well-being and that you feel connected with the essence of the tree. It has been my profound experience that, with the exception of fully grown oaks, all trees love to be acknowledged and given small gifts. Ancient oaks seem to give off an air of indifference and superiority that is difficult to penetrate.

You will discover that each tree has certain attributes that it brings to the month and you should consider this as the year progresses. The silver birch for example, is the first tree to re-populate an area after a clearing or a forest fire: hence, it is the tree of new beginnings. However, you need to combine silver birch with alder, the dreaming tree, to make a powerful combination for thinking of new plans and carrying them out.

Each moon-month can be seen to have attributes that we can bring into our daily life. If we do the appropriate things at these times, nature will magnify our own desires and energies to make whatever we achieve more profound and yet easier to manage. For example, hawthorn is the tree for mid-spring. It stands for purity and cleansing. Its flowers are predominantly white. This is the time for spring-cleaning, opening the house and airing carpets and bed linen after the enclosed stuffiness of winter.

The trees acquire their attributes in three main ways. First, as we saw with silver birch, their own natural characteristics can be applied to other areas of life. Holly, for example, has sharp leaves to protect its berries in winter, but in the summer the leaves are soft and pliable. So, we can say that holly is highly protective of her own but in the summer is laid-back and placid.

Sometimes it is less obvious attributes that are used. The alder appears to bleed when it is cut, as its resin is a rich red. This made it sacred to the Celt but also linked it with death. Because of this and its highly oiled wood, coffins were often made of alder wood so the dreaming tree became sinister and feared.

Second, trees gained meanings from the gods associated with them. Odin, for example, was said to have hung upside-down from the branches of an ash while he was given insight into the runes. Often portrayed as the tree of life, the ash reaches high into the sky and deep into the ground. Its supple white wood was thought excellent by the Celts for making spears, which connected it with the Celtic god Lugh, the great warrior, who carried a magical ash spear. If you wish to gain attributes of power and energy, determination and even aggression, ash is the wood to use.

Third, there is the spiritual aspect of the tree. This is the aspect of tree-work that is most attractive: you can read all the books but it is only when you meet the trees that you truly begin to understand their beauty, grace, and inner knowledge.

I only came to grasp this through my work with the silver birches. By meditating with them and, perhaps as importantly, just watching and being with them, I came to understand and appreciate them. The silver birch is sometimes called 'the nervous tree' because its leaves quiver all the time, but I think 'the dancing tree' would be more appropriate. One of my friends suggested that the trees attracted any breath of wind that was flowing by. And it is true: all the other trees in a valley might be still in the summer heat, but the silver birch dances and shimmers, its leaves twirling and weaving in some breeze it has summoned.

This view of the silver birch offers a more positive, self-assured image of the tree. Often when I go past them without stopping on the other side of the pond, the sound of the wind whistling through their branches attracts my attention. Then it seems as if they are cheerfully waving to me, as a friend would.

It is all too easy to anthropomorphise trees. At the end of the day, they are only plants, they cannot see or hear you, but they are to be venerated because many are so old. Anything that lives for hundreds of years should be respected and acknowledged, but trees have no intelligence as we understand it. They do, however, have presence. They are inspiring and challenging. Trees enrich our lives and we should give thanks for that.

WORKING WITH TREES IN GENERAL

You need know nothing about the legends associated with or the attributes of a tree to work with it. All you need is to know that you are drawn to it and want to spend time with it.

You may already have trees that feel special to you. If not, take a walk somewhere convenient where there are several. As you approach each tree, consider how it would feel to sit under it. Would it feel good? Would you feel as if you were imposing? Perhaps you don't feel anything. Carry on until you find a tree. The chances are that you will know it immediately. It will feel right. Often there will be another sign: a white feather, for example, or a natural dip in the land that creates a seat. One old beech tree I came across in Yorkshire had a large root that formed a perfect bench right against its trunk.

Or you could buy a set of tree cards. Some are straightforward information cards but others, like *The Celtic Tree Oracle*, have divinatory uses. Select the pictures of trees native to your area, then place the cards face down on the table in front of you. Close your eyes and say aloud, 'Help me, my guardian angels and spirits. Help me know which tree I should work with.' As you say this, pass your hand over the cards. Almost at once you should feel that one of the cards is different from the others: it may seem to radiate heat or cold. Sometimes I feel anothers' hand push mine on to a card.

Or, as you gather knowledge about the local trees in your neighbourhood, collect a memento from each. Remember never to harm a tree – there are always twigs or cones lying about. Carefully label each memento with coloured thread, then pop them into a cotton bag. Now when you want to go and work with a tree you can select one with ease and carry the memento with you, establishing a relationship even before you arrive.

Some like to collect wands from trees and you will hear them say that they asked the tree before they lopped off a branch. One of my friends was at a retreat centre where they were building a sweat lodge during their ceremonies. They were all sent off to find trees happy to be chopped down. Of course, it is a moot point as to whether you'd want to make a shelter, or a wand, from suicidal wood.

Once you have found your tree, develop a relationship with it. The easiest way to do this is just to spend time with it. Sit under its branches and enjoy the space, or read. Maybe you could paint or sketch it. Touch the tree and feel the texture of its bark. As you stand or sit there you will come to realise that the trunk is moving. Except on the calmest of summer days, trees move constantly. To become aware of its movement is a sign that you are really paying attention to the tree.

The next step is to imagine that you are a tree, like the one you have chosen. Sit quietly with your back to it and look about. Imagine what it would be like to be as tall and old as this tree. Imagine having roots deep in the earth holding you steady and firm. Feel your branches reaching up into the sky and out across the land. Feel the sun on your leaves and the contented warmth spreading through you.

Think what it would be like to have no sight, hearing, taste, or smell. You would simply be. Perhaps you can sense the other trees around you and take some comfort from their presence.

Simply being. Feeling the sun and moon pass overhead, wind and rain, sunshine and showers, snow and ice, all coming and going while you grow to the sun.

Think of all of this as you sit by your companion and wonder if you would like to be a tree.

Take time to tend the tree. Clear away any ivy growing up the trunk. The easiest way to do this is to cut it at the base. Because this seems cruel to the ivy, which is only doing what it naturally does, I cut most but not all the tendrils. The alternative is to nip off the top before it gets too high to reach. Also, pay attention to soil erosion and changing ground conditions. If the tree prefers wet, soggy ground, like alder, willow or silver birch, make sure it isn't getting too dry. Build dykes to prevent the soil being washed away. You will find that the more you tend your trees, the better you get to know them, and you will feel them getting used to you.

USING TREES WHILE MEDITATING

Once you feel you have established a relationship with the tree, you can use it while you meditate. All plants can sense, in some way, the different energies that we humans give off. This is how they recognise us. Experiments show that plants can distinguish who feeds or prunes them and they act accordingly.

So, take time to win the trust of your tree. When you meditate your energy levels change – you are probably already well aware of that and you should let the tree get used to it as well. Take some time to meditate beside the tree. Use the exercises as before. You may find that as you send your roots down into the land, you will become aware of other roots from the trees around you. That is fine, but make sure you avoid them.

As a variation on the normal meditation form, hold a piece of wood from your chosen tree and as you pull the earth and cleanse with the light, include the wood in the process. Dead wood only has an echo of the vibrancy and life of living wood, but it is a gentle start for you and you can use it both beside the tree and with meditations at home.

You should only proceed to the next meditation after you have meditated beside the tree twenty or thirty times.

Meditation With Trees
Make your sign to start spiritual work and follow the Meditation Exercise. Once you are floating, sense the energies of the tree

beside you. You should be able to feel them. Feel your body full of light energy, turn slowly and reach out your hand until you feel the outer energies of the tree. Depending on the tree and its age, this might only be an inch or so from the bark. This movement is difficult to do as you need to maintain your inner eye, all aspects of yourself focused inwards, while at the same time moving your body. It will feel like moving a lumbering piece of machinery and it may take you several attempts to achieve this.

Eventually, you will be able to see yourself as a light-being stroking the energies of the tree and, at the same time, be doing it physically. This is a great moment.

Now, with both hands connecting to the energies of the tree, feel your aura and that of the tree merge. This is a slow and special process. You are effectively becoming part of the tree or, more importantly, the tree is becoming part of you. As this happens, seek out the properties of the tree that you feel you need and let them flow into you. Slowly, in return, feed love into the tree. If at any point in this operation you feel resistance, stop. This has to be something that happens willingly on both sides.

Feel the energies flow round you. You are in the tree and yet you are separate. You are branch and leaf, yet you are skin and bone. You are old and silent, you are young and noisy.

Now gradually separate again and pull back physically too. Feel the white light of love pour down through your crown and bathe your whole body in its healing, purity. Feel it flow right through you and into the ground. Now pull up the wholesome, enriching earth energies and fill your body with its pulsing energy.

Repeat the cleansing with the white light and then, when you are filled with it, stop and notice how cleansed and pure you are.

Stand like this for a couple of minutes, then feel your physical side returning. Feel your fingers and toes, sense the blood pulsing in your veins and saliva in your mouth. Now, when you *are ready, make the sign to end your spiritual work, and open your eyes.*

When you look around, everything will seem strangely green and oddly different from before. This is a powerful meditation and you should expect to take several hours to recover your equilibrium. It is also a most delicious and inspiring exercise.

WORKING IN THE SACRED GROVE

Just as we are attracted to the trees, so are spirits. Just as different trees give off different energies, so different spirits are attracted to different trees. All of this reinforces the power that we can harness to help ourselves become more spiritually aware. Mythical characters have been associated with particular trees and we can use the Celtic sagas to understand some of the properties and powers these trees inspire. Baile and Ailinn were royal lovers but doomed through the ministrations of a ghostly enemy. Each died believing the other to be already dead. A yew tree grew from the head of Baile's grave that bore the image of his lover, and from Ailinn's an apple tree whose fruit bore Baile's.

While the tale is sad it has a happy ending, of sorts. Two hundred years later when Airt 'the lonely' ordered that all the wands of love songs that had been carved from the two trees be brought to the high king of Ireland's stronghold at Tara, the wood leaped together and could not be parted by might or magic. Airt commanded that they be considered part of the treasure of Tara.

From this tale we can see the yew as male and the apple as female. Yew was for the heir to the throne of Ulster, while apple was for the granddaughter of the king of Leinster who had to make a choice of lover. There is also, of course, an element of rebirth and renewal, of ultimate success. If we want to do any work based on relationships we can use yew for the male aspect and apple for the female.

Where trees grow in the wild, natural clearings form. Over time, paths become established, apparently weaving indiscriminately between the trees but in fact following complex flows of energies in the land. Even in plantations where the trees are set closely together in rows, you'll notice that the paths are never regular: nature will always win out. Even if a path is laid in a straight line, those who use it will often take a different route that feels more comfortable.

Sometimes the clearings will just emerge, despite the best efforts of the planters. There may appear to be no difference between a clearing and a grove, but there is. A clearing is simply a spot in the woods that is clear of trees, for whatever reason. A grove is formed by the trees. They crowd around the open space but are unable or unwilling to enter it. That is because they are held back. The sense of a presence that keeps the ground clear is what makes a grove such a magical place. To enter a grove is to trespass on the power of that space, so you should never do so without permission. Once in a sacred grove, remember that you are there on sufferance. Be respectful at all times and do not seek out the spirits of the grove – if they wish it, they will come to you.

Sacred Grove Meditation

Before you enter a sacred grove stop and ask permission. To do this, stand still and close your eyes. Seek to empty your mind of all thoughts and awareness of the trees and spirits around you. Then ask, 'Spirits and Beings of the Sacred Grove, may I enter?' Wait to see if you get a reply, if not repeat it. Do not worry if this takes several minutes and many attempts. You are surrounded by powerful trees and it will be difficult for you to clear your mind.

If, after many attempts, you have not had a reply, do not enter. To enter a sacred grove without permission is to breach the hospitality of the spirits, and while nothing horrible would happen, your attempts at meditation would probably fail.

Almost certainly you will be given permission. Now move slowly into the grove. You may wish to give the spirits a small gift, some food, perhaps. Now find a spot within the grove that you find comfortable. Try facing different ways and move about until you feel you are connecting with the energy of the land.

Look about you and see the different kinds of trees and bushes growing there. If you don't know all their names, don't worry. See them for what they are. Are they tall or short? Jagged or smooth? What is their trunk like? Are their leaves long or short? Take time with each and enjoy seeing it. Then pick one or two trees that you feel particularly drawn to and spend some time examining them in great detail – try to notice the smallest things.

Mark the line around the grove and, as you look about, see in your mind's eye a white line that marks the boundary of the sacred grove. Now make the sign for starting your spiritual work, and do the Meditation Exercise. As you send your roots down and bring the energies into your body always be aware of the presence of the trees around you. See them as vague shadows on the horizon with the trees you picked out as a stronger presence.

Now you are floating. Be aware of the trees crowding around the grove. But here you are clear of their energies. The grove holds them back and lets you enjoy the essence of their energies and attributes but keeps the psychic space that you need to breathe. This is what is so precious about a sacred grove: not only are you free and secure, the echo of the trees that surround it gives off a subtle but powerful profile that we can use.

For example, if the trees that surrounded a sacred grove are oak and beech, then that grove would be a very special spot in which to make sense of ideas you have been studying or teachings you are trying to comprehend. If the main trees are alder and willow, then the grove would be a great place for contemplation and dreaming.

As you float, open and trusting, feel the subtle energies you are seeking wash over you. Attract the powers you need, and feel them come to you. If you need courage, feel the holly tree reaching out to you. If you need energy, feel the bramble shoots come to you.

When you are ready, release all these ideas and feel yourself free again, floating. Slowly come back to where you are. Feel your fingers and toes. Open your eyes and make your sign to close spiritual work. When you are finished, remember to thank the site, and once you are out of the grove, turn back and bow in respect.

The sacred grove is a special place because it allows you to work with the energies of various trees from a distance. Sometimes you need that freedom. Feel your own spirits around you and feel them relaxing and exploring this remarkable space too. In a place of tranquillity and calm, you are safe and protected.

This sense of security is something we rarely experience. It is precious and should be used sparingly. Otherwise we risk returning too often until the special powers of the place are lost on us.

Remember, trees are more than tools to help you in your meditation and self-awareness work. They are living beings with their own right to life and must be given the respect that all living creatures are due. With their spirits they can help you explore issues that you need either to resolve or free yourself from. How lucky we are that we can spend an afternoon under the spreading canopy of an oak tree and call it work.

12

STORYTELLING –
TALES OF THE FAERY FOLK

Imagine the scene. The whole *clachan* has gathered to hear the Druid speak. After a communal meal and much drinking, the head of the village calls for silence. There is an immediate hush and, in that heavy moment of expectation, children gather near their parents, women huddle together and the men sit back, all ready to enjoy the tale.

The Druid is a consummate actor. He has been trained for twenty years and has that again in experience. Without saying a word he has the audience enthralled. He steps towards the fire and slowly looks around. The villagers barely breathe as the tension builds.

They already know the story. Some will have heard it many times, word for word, action by action, voice by voice. Yet they all gasp as he reveals the treachery, they sigh when the lovers meet, and even some of the men have tears in their eyes as the Druid takes them to the site of the hero's death in the arms of his beloved.

For the Celts, storytelling was more than entertainment. Storytellers were trained by the greatest Druids of the day to take the sagas to the people. Every line and nuance had to be learned by heart, every gesture and inflection practised again and again.

Words were powerful to the Celt. You could not write them down – to trap a word on paper was to lose control over it. Consider how a note in the voice or a carefully chosen phrase not only conveys a message but a whole range of emotions and subtleties. 'He was your friend!' said in a hurt tone might mean,

'How can you say such a thing about someone you called a friend?' 'He was your friend' said indignantly means 'How could you possibly be friends with someone who behaves so badly?'

And, of course, when you write it down, you do lose control. Two different people will read any sentence differently, take different meanings from it and react to it in different ways.

It is certain that the Druids knew of writing and may even have used it. We know they taught ancient Greek and later Latin in their seminaries, so it would be wrong to think that they were noble savages as later classical Roman authors tried to portray them. The Druids *chose* not to write anything down. It was not that they lacked the ability to do so.

Storytelling takes various forms. Among the most revered story-tellers were the poets. One of the most famous semi-mythical of them was Taliesin, whose name comes down to us today through some of his own poems and Celtic sagas. The poets were thought to be particularly close to the other worlds and many would retreat to dark caves or tunnels to compose their poems, leaving behind the distractions of this world. Such was the power of these men and women that they could bring down kings with a play on words, so they were celebrated and feared probably in equal measure.

It was thought that their inspiration came from the spirits that surrounded them and the gods and goddesses they could work with. The spirits struggle to compress their complex ideas into our vocabulary. Poems might be deceptively simple yet stunningly complex. So, poetry was not something to listen to with half an ear. It required full attention and a lot of thought afterwards. Even the poet may not understand all the nuances of their poem.

Writing a Poem

Do not fear the emptiness of a clear page, welcome it. Follow this exercise, then take some time to try to understand what you have written.

Sit in your Sacred Space and do the Sitting Simply exercise.

Once you are completely relaxed and focused on yourself, take up your journal and hold a pen ready to write.

Seek out the spirits that are all around you. Try to feel their presence. Hold that sense of them being there while you light a candle. Now say, 'With this candle, I welcome my spirits. With this candle, I thank you for the light. Guide me, spirits, help me, let the light inspire me.'

See yourself sitting before a great white flame in a darkened cave. There is dry earth on the floor and you can just make out the stone walls beyond the light of the flame. You are not alone: spirits seem to fill the space around you. You are all gathered around the sacred flame.

Now when you look at the fire you can see a great stone Celtic cross emerging from the flames. Look closely at it. See how it is weathered with age, mottled with lichen and moss. There seem to be strange patterns in the moss: you strain to see the pictures they paint.

Now the flame has faded into the background, although you can still feel its heat, and you listen to the spirits whispering in your ear. As you continue to study the cross, listen to what they say. Remember, sometimes the words are not there to hear but, rather, to feel. Inside your mind you sense cogs turning and ideas coming to fruition.

Feel the gates of inspiration opening and, when you are ready, take up your pen and write whatever comes into your head. Don't worry about spelling, grammar or structure, or whether it makes sense. Don't even take note of whether it is in English. Just write.

Write everything that comes to mind. If words fail you, sketch or draw what you see. If it is coming too fast, write down the key words so that you can come back and fill in the gaps.

Just write. This creation is so exciting and rewarding. It can be highly emotional and sometimes very personal. But that is perfect. This form of creativity is something that everyone can do. You don't need years of training or degrees and certificates. You only need a pen and paper.

When you have finished, go back over what you have written, tidy and polish it. This may take some time and you may want to leave it for several days, then return to it. Always keep the original scribbles because later, when the time is right, you may wish to work out how you got to the final copy. However, be aware that sometimes when you try to improve your work you lose the spontaneity and clarity of the original thoughts.

STORYTELLING

Storytelling is creative too. The great storytellers of their day would, of course, compose new stories and improve existing ones, but their main role was the retelling of the Celtic sagas. The sagas were a great way of educating people, of passing on information and inspiring them to great deeds. After all, what young boy would not dream of being the great hero Cúchulainn? Women would yearn for the beauty of Aine or the love of Baile.

There is another side too. Storytellers might be seen as the spin-doctors of their time, telling tales of the daring deeds of the hero-king and his great army, of dastardly treachery by the dastardly enemy and the noble sacrifices of the Druids.

Storytellers also used their craft to explain why things were as they were and how they came about. So, like the poets, the storytellers were of great importance and powerful in their domain. As Druids, they owned nothing and wished for nothing but they were still tied to certain families or geographical areas and could not necessarily be seen as independent of the world around them, without views or opinions.

Even today it is rare that we pass on news without adding something to it. Normally we make a drama of it, savouring each part of the adventure until the end is revealed. It is fun and a key part of social interaction.

Children love storytellers. Despite television, cartoons and DVDs there is something intimate and engrossing about a storyteller gathering together a group of young children to hear stories of heroes and monsters.

The vast majority of adults seem to have almost lost the art of telling stories and listening. Perhaps we are too sophisticated, these days, or have mislaid the ability to create the necessary inner landscapes. The one exception seems to be ghost stories. As a student I lived for a year in an old tenement flat that was, as they say, full of atmosphere. At night we would often find ourselves sitting downstairs telling ghost stories. All around us the room would darken as, one by one, we told our tales. Through the dark hours we huddled together around the fire, revelling in the reality of the ghostly realms.

Ghost stories are still popular, and appeal to the Celt particularly because they stimulate the sixth sense. They resonate with us and remind us that there is much more to this world than we can see and hear, touch, smell and taste.

THE TUATHA DÉ DANAAN

One of the most vital and vivid of the legends told by the storytellers was of the history of Ireland and the peoples who lived there before the Celts arrived. It was widely known that the Celts were travellers and not of the sacred isle. The ancient tract The Book of Invasions, included by Christian monks in the collection known as the Book of Leinster, tells us that when the Celts arrived in Ireland they found that people were already there, a tribe of gods called the Tuatha dé Danaan, literally 'the people of the Goddess Danu'. Almost unbelievably the gods were unable to repel the Celts: the land of Ireland was sympathetic to the usurpers. Eventually a great parley was called with both sides present and the Druids constructed a compromise. As part of this deal the Tuatha dé Danaan left the material land of Ireland and went to the spiritual or underworld, leaving the mountains, rivers and forests to the Celts.

However, the working of this accord proved more difficult than might at first appear because the Gods and Goddesses of the Danu still had their divine attributes and could use them to help or hinder the Celts. They could, for example, control the weather or the sea: they could help crops grow and cattle to fatten; or they could starve the people and destroy their livelihood. And so a second treaty was drawn up between the Celts and the Danaan, one that is now lost to us but which seems to have committed the Danaan to helping, or at least not hindering, the Celt in return for homage and offerings.

The Tuatha dé Danaan are still in Ireland and have become, to us, the Faery Folk: a people who live close to us and yet are not of us. A people whose destiny depends on us but who can work with or against us. A people who think like us and behave like us, yet are different, with different values and abilities. It is a complex and baffling relationship.

The stories of the Danaan are legendary and as time has gone on they have been recast as ancient kings and queens, gods and goddesses and, of course, faeries. For us the important point is that the tales are so definite: they explain where the Tuatha dé Danaan are from; why they are in Ireland and why we should pay homage to them. But it was a two-way process. Homage was paid for specific reasons: this was not worship or sacrifice, it was payment. In other words, the Tuatha were not a possibility or a belief, they were a fact. Every Celt knew they existed and that they were capable of good or indifference.

However tempting it might be for the Western scientist in all of us to dismiss such talk of Faery Folk as fancy, we must bear in mind that legends explain something that people can see. For example, the ancient Celts in Scotland practised, in some form, a matriarchal society where title and wealth passed through the female side. This was relatively unusual and to explain it a legend was born. It said that when the Irish first arrived in Scotland around AD 500 they found that the Picts were already there but had few women. The Irish sold them some of their own women-folk, but their price was that the family's name and wealth had to pass down the female line. This also helped to explain why the Picts and the Celts were so similar and intermarriage so common.

So, here the legends of the Tuatha dé Danaan were necessary because of people's personal experiences of the Danaan. Perhaps they saw them on the shore of the loch at sunset, or heard their thin horns in the woods at night. Maybe the kings and chief druids even met Danaan ambassadors.

What we can be certain of is that the Danaan existed for the Celts and were so much part of the landscape that they had to be explained.

Legends of the Faery Folk exist throughout the Celtic lands and further afield. In Scotland, for example, many sites are associated with the Faeries. Some people in rural areas still leave out tributes at certain times of the year. When I was a child it was believed that if you left out a broken tool at night the Brownies would mend it if they could.

As late as 1690 Robert Kirk, a Scottish Episcopalian minister, wrote one of the classic books on Faerylore *The Secret Commonwealth of Elves, Fauns and Fairies*. In it he outlined their lives, told of how they would kidnap women to suckle their children, and mentioned someone he knew to whom this had happened.

These faeries, however, were not the delicate Tinkerbells so favoured by Victorians; rather, they were beings so like us that they could pass in our streets and not be noticed. Kirk's book is all the more remarkable because he was talking of the times in which he lived, of people who lived around him and of events and occurrences that most knew of.

The apparent reality of the Tuatha dé Danaan is a challenge to us, but it is also a reminder that we need to understand the spiritual realms around us to comprehend anything about where and how we lead our lives.

USING STORIES TO IMPROVE OUR LIVES

Storytelling can make us more aware of the world we live in. One day when you are out for a walk choose a bush or tree, maybe even a flower. Stop and examine it in some detail: see how it is growing and what is nearby. Is it thriving or struggling to survive? Gather as much information as you can.

After a few visits allow yourself some extra time to sit with your flower and try to feel what it feels: the sun on its leaves, the wind through its petals. Sense what it senses: can it feel your presence? Is it afraid of you? Does it recognise you from earlier visits? Try to understand how it would feel to be this living creature.

From this empathy, start to build up a story of its life. Little by little allow the spirits to whisper to you. Listen to the sounds on the breeze and construct a story. You could write it down in your journal, but sometimes it is better to hold it in your head. Each time you pass, seek out the flower and tell yourself its story, perhaps adding more detail or new facts. Gradually you will realise that your story seems real. And that is because, in some ways, it is.

Storytelling is fun and it helps you remember, for example, what plants are growing in any area, or how a particular tree looked six months ago. It's strange but true that we seem more able to remember stories than facts. Telling yourself stories can also serve practical purposes. Sometimes at night if I can't sleep, I lie in bed and tell myself a story. If I'm stressed at work or need distraction, I will dream up stories.

When we were young we did this all the time. We would play together and every sentence would begin, 'Let's make it that . . .' or 'Let's pretend that . . .' and then we would act out our stories. Sometimes as adults we can be too sophisticated for our own good.

The great Celtic sagas were much more than they seemed. Even after they were Christianised by the first Celtic monks, there was still much in them that is worthy of our interest. To illustrate this, consider the tale of the boy Cúchulainn. When he first arrived at the court of King Conchubar at Emain Macha, near Armagh in Ulster, he found a hurling match under way and immediately joined in, scoring a goal. Only then did the players realise there was a stranger in their midst. 'But this cannot be!' they cried, and strove to drive the small boy off the field. Cúchulainn wrestled with them and put up a good show for himself.

Such was the noise that the son of the king came out. When he saw all the boys fighting on one and that one beating them off, he laughed and applauded the stranger. 'Come!' he cried. 'The king shall hear of this.'

From this story we can learn the importance of not leaping in without checking: Cúchulainn had joined a match that was banned to those who were not of the camp. That he fought back when the other boys tried to eject him made the situation worse, not better as might at first appear. The story also shows that one person can take on many if they believe right is on their side. Cúchulainn thought the others were breaking the convention of hospitality and courtesy to a stranger. Had he known he was in the wrong, he tells the king, he would not have fought so vigorously.

There are even personal lessons in it to be learned: no one is allowed to play who has not already been accepted into the camp. This might have a parallel with our own spiritual development: it is a warning that if we rush in and work with the spirits without understanding what we are doing then we disrupt rather than heal, destroy rather than help.

Now, of course it is possible to argue that you can over-analyse a situation and sometimes a story is just a story. But that is to miss the point: like a work of art or a skilfully carved abstract sculpture, a story can be a tool to help us examine our own situation and shortcomings. It can even reveal to us a way forward, and perhaps inspire us to greater things.

Story Writing Exercise

The Celts loved stories with hidden meanings. Every story, they believed, had three levels. First, there was the literal meaning:

that what you heard was what had happened. Then there was the simile: that the whole story was meant to make them think of something in their own life or experience. In the third, or metaphorical, reading, you may divine a hidden message in the story.

Try this exercise. It's fun to hide meanings in what you say. It's also easier to work backwards. Let's imagine that you have a partner who doesn't give you enough affection. Fill in the space below with a literal meaning, then write a short story for them.

Hidden meaning: love opens your soul to the winds of the universe.

Simile: opening a door and stepping into the sunshine.

Literal:

The story need be no longer than, say, 800 words. The trick is not to try to be too clever or obtuse: there is little point in writing a message so dense that no one can decipher its meaning. Like Paulo Coelho's The Alchemist or Kahlil Gibran's The Prophet, some of the best stories ever written are those that appear simple.

So, storytelling is far more than simple enjoyment. Unlike so much of our anodyne entertainment today, a good story can explain things to us, teach us about the world we live in and lead us further along our spiritual path. It can of course also be a ripping good yarn!

13

MORE ADVANCED MEDITATION TECHNIQUES

The art of meditation is a lifelong learning experience. In Chapter Three, I outlined the basic technique, and that most powerful meditation exercise should remain the core of your meditation. However, there are tools you can use to enhance the experience.

The reason we meditate is to help change our point of focus from the material world and its concerns to the spiritual world and its magical awareness. The more you meditate, the more you retune your mind to the spiritual dimension. And the more you do that, the less important the petty annoyances of everyday life become, which helps you achieve increasingly insightful meditation. It is a wheel that, once it begins to roll, gathers momentum. That is one of the reasons why opening and closing ceremonies are so important: if you failed to do that, it is possible that the inner focus of your meditation would break out into everyday life, which would be dangerous if you were driving a car, tending children or even shopping.

USING MUSIC

Most people discover the magical beauty of Celtic music, long before they discover Celtic Spirituality. As Jessica Powers wrote:

> I ask and ask, but no-one ever tells me
> What place I go when I meet Gaelic music
> And we are left a little while alone

Something in the music sings to the soul, whether it is ancient or modern. A door opens on to another world where emotions are pure and love is languid.

To the Celt, music was a powerful tool. Perhaps accompanied by poetry, it was the key to the heart of man. The harpists that wandered the roads of Ireland were treated like lords and it was considered a great honour, well into the late Middle Ages, to have such a bard attend your house. Like the *file*, the bards played from a great repertoire of memorised songs as well as their own compositions.

To witness the power of music, visit your local super-market or indoor shopping centre. Many play music: they know that by filling the silence with pleasant sounds, shoppers are more comfortable in their surroundings, which means they will spend more. But the effects of music can be more subtle: experi-ments run in a major supermarket chain in England showed that when they played French classical music, they sold more French wine, and when they played German music, they sold more German wine. This hints at the pull music has for us so use it with care.

Meditating With Music

Place a CD in your player and line up the track you want to hear. If you have headphones, you may like to use them. Then sit in your Sacred Space with the remote control and do the Sitting Simply exercise. Once you are calm and floating gently, turn on the music. Concentrate on it and let it take you where it will. Soar over the mountains, plunge into the gullies; dance with the gods and weep with the widow. Let the music unlock your innermost emotions and welcome the release.

When the music stops, switch off the machine and sit quietly. Make the sign to close spiritual work. Try to work out why you dreamed what you did. Why did the music make you go where you went, see what you saw, remember what you remembered? What did you need to understand? What secrets were revealed

*to you? Take some time to consider all of this, then write down
in your journal the music you listened to, the dreams you had
and what you think it all meant.*

In this context music can be a cleanser, allowing emotions
from our subconscious to surface and, in releasing them, begin
the process of getting rid of them. If you cannot understand why
you dreamed what you did, then leave it for now. Return to it in
a few days and try again.

Of course, sometimes it is not a release but an inspiration.
Sometimes the music will reveal places you need to be or actions
you must take. After the music has ended, you will not feel pensive
or thoughtful but keen to get on. You will feel invigorated and
excited.

You can invoke different meditative experiences by altering
your choice of music. As you try different pieces, notice how
they affect you. In the future you will be able to select music that
is particularly good for, say, remembering your ancestors, over-
coming frustration or de-stressing and relaxing.

Shamanic workers often use drum beats when they are meditating. The regular rhythm can be reproduced with voices, bells
or almost anything that is to hand. It induces a trance-like
state, which helps the shaman to travel to the healing worlds
and, more importantly, shows him the path home. You can buy
CDs with a single drum beat on tracks that run for fifteen to
thirty minutes, which will help you regulate the time of your
journey.

For the Celts ritual music would have tied in with the major
festivals of the year. Although we cannot know for sure, we can
be fairly certain that these festivals would have gone on for
several days with huge fires, dancing, singing, music and storytelling and drug-taking. They were times to leave behind the
responsibilities of day-to-day life and enter a magical, carefree
world. We can only guess at how wild and bacchanalian such
festivals were.

USING CRYSTALS

For the Celt crystals were seen as gifts from the earth. More than that, they were tools with the power to bring the other worlds and this world closer together. You can see this at the Newgrange Neolithic burial mound at Brú na Bóinne in central Ireland where the quartz that originally covered the outside has been restored to create an amazing white wall that is visible from a long way off. More than that it creates a sort of barrier as you approach: you can feel the energy of the crystals pushing you back. To a people who were aware of the subtleties of earth energy, this barrier would have been powerful and alarming: it would have felt as if the gods of the site were pushing them away – and who would want to ignore the wishes of the gods?

Legends tell of Merlin's crystal cave, a small space he could crawl into and be totally surrounded by quartz. It was there that his powers of prophecy were unlocked and to there that he returned for healing and renewal.

We can use this same energy to enhance our meditations. Crystals come in all colours, shapes and sizes. It is more than likely that the Druids and Celtic saints would have had access to a wide range of gems and crystals and would have used them for decoration and spiritual work.

To begin with you should seek some quartz. Quartz crystal is clear or opaque and comes either as a tumblestone, shiny and smooth, or unpolished. You can find it in almost any New Age or New Age-inspired gift shop. Use your intuition to select a piece, ideally a larger piece that you can hold in both hands. They are not expensive and, after all, your quartz may well be with you for the rest of your life so price should not be an issue.

Take time to find the right piece – it took me a couple of years to find the wand I currently have. I looked on and off for a long time, picking up beautiful pieces of quartz but not feeling any connection, until one day, I saw the wand and knew right away that it was the one for me, even before I picked it up. Interestingly it wasn't the most beautiful piece and other people have told me this too; the piece that is meant for you can seem quite ordinary, though others will often see its beauty.

Looking After Your Crystals

Having a crystal in the house is a little like owning a pet. Lots of people are ready with advice, but you will get to know your crystal yourself and listen to what it needs, see how it responds and act accordingly.

Now, of course some people will be highly sceptical of this and tell you that a rock is a rock is a rock. But quartz is special. We have already seen how certain spirits are attracted to certain sites. The same principle is true here: powerful spirits, who can be of a great help to us, are attracted to powerful crystals.

Finding a Name For Your Crystal

To listen to your crystal, you will need to find a name for it. To do this, go to your Sacred Space and sit holding it in both hands. Do your sign to start spiritual work and then the Sitting Simply exercise. Now, when you are ready, become aware of the crystal in your hands. Feel it cold against your palms. Sense it as an entity on its own.

Now imagine a small glowing ball of white energy in your right palm. Feel it within your hand, glowing. Feel the glow extend slowly up your arm until you can sense a white line stretching from your palm to your shoulder. Now feel it move behind your neck and down your other arm until the white light is stretching from your right palm in an arc to your left palm. Feel that light with certainty. Now feel it pressing against your crystal. Try to pass it through the crystal. Ask permission from the crystal and sense it opening up to you. Feel the energy pulse from your right hand over your shoulders, down your left arm, through the crystal and complete the circle. Feel that pulse move faster and faster until there is just the white band from hand to hand.

Now sense the crystal again. You are connected by the white light and the crystal is happy to be working with you. Feel the comradeship of the two of you united in purpose and energy. Focus on the crystal while keeping the white light going and, aloud, ask the crystal its name.

When I did this exercise, I suppose I was expecting Fred or Robert or something like that, but what I got, very clearly, was a moving symbol, which I knew instantly was the right name. It is not something that can be said aloud – at least, not in any language I know.

The name is important because it is the key to opening up the crystal, so it is best that you do not tell anyone else or even write it down. If you want to put it into your journal, try to disguise it so that no one else can find it.

Now that you have the name, welcome the crystal into your home and your life. Thank it for choosing you and promise to look after and care for it. By tuning into the crystal, you can find out whether it wants to be cleansed, where to store it, how to use it, and even whether other people should handle it.

You may wish to talk to your crystal and tell it something of yourself, your household and your family. When you are ready, stop the white light circle and become aware again of your surroundings. Feel the gap between you and your crystal. In due course open your eyes and make the sign for ending spiritual work.

If you find you are unable to open the crystal, or a name does not come to you, don't worry. Sometimes it takes time to tune in to the wavelength of a crystal. Just do this exercise once a week and it will happen – and be all the more rewarding because of the extra work you have had to do.

Crystals need to be cleansed regularly and this is best done in running water, preferably a burn or a small waterfall. Just as static gathers dust, a crystal may attract debris that blocks it and prevents it working properly.

Views differ on where it is best to store crystals. Some therapists feel that if they are left in the sun, they can be overcharged and eventually be useless. Others believe the more sunlight the better. Everyone, it seems, agrees that moonlight is good for crystals and you should let them bathe in the full moon every few months. But, as in all things, your crystal will let you know.

Meditating with Crystals

Crystals serve several different purposes for us when we are meditating. Like music, they can inspire us. As we sit and look into them, we can see worlds within worlds, realms within realms. Large pieces of fluorite look like forest glades with light filtering through the dark green foliage of the trees to reveal winding paths weaving through the green and pale purple landscape. Quartz shows us shadows of angels and spirits, reflecting back to us images of purity and inspiration. These inner worlds can take us far from our day-to-day lives to places we have never been and worlds we never knew existed.

Crystal Protection Exercise

Crystals can also help us focus on ourselves during meditation by preventing other influences coming near us. To use crystals in this way, make the sign to start your spiritual work, then follow the Finding a Name for Your Crystal exercise outlined above. Once you are connected with your crystal begin the Meditation Exercise (page 33), taking care to pull up the earth energy, then cleanse yourself and the crystal with the white light.

Now when you are floating feel the energy of the crystal in your hand and see, in your mind's eye, a wall of crystal bricks being built around you, about three feet distant, until you are surrounded by them. You are safe within this area: the extra power from the crystal is combining with your own energy to create this space just for you.

As you become more adept at using the crystal and more familiar with it, you can control the building of this wall, or perhaps put in windows to allow you to see out. I found this particularly helpful at sacred sites because you can be easily distracted by the mass of spiritual activity in those places. It is often fun to meet ancient spirits or see old village scenes, but ultimately it is a distraction.

Eventually the crystal will be so in tune with you that it will build the wall or lower it without you being aware of the need for it. I used to find this distracting. On one occasion, in my mind's eye, I saw that I was surrounded by a dozen monks, who seemed to be jeering at me. Before I could react, the crystal wall went up. I never saw them again or even sensed their presence at that particular site. Clearly it is for your own good, but it can be frustrating.

When you are ready to finish, stop the white line and become aware of your own body and surroundings. Thank the crystal, then see the white light washing through your body again but not through the crystal. Fill your body with it. Feel your whole being glow with white light and also, most importantly, feel the distance between you and your crystal. Now make the sign for stopping your spiritual work.

USING IMAGES AND SYMBOLS

For humans, visual stimulation is very powerful, and images can be helpful in the meditative process. Paintings, drawings and photos that you have created are especially powerful: they invoke memories of the occasion and the act of their creation.

Similarly symbols are more than their shape: they can carry information, emotion and power. Take the symbol of the Christian Church: the cross or crucifix is recognised around the world and conjures up the story of Jesus Christ.

Meditation Exercise with Images
To use an image in meditation, start by making the sign for spiritual work. Sitting in your sacred space, hold the image in your

hands or place it in front of you where you can see it easily and clearly. Now gaze at it. If it is of a place, imagine (or remember) being there. Feel the cool wind on your face as you paddle along the edge of the loch; sense the age and veneration of the mountains; hear the laughter from the burn as it dances past you.

If you've chosen an abstract picture, study the colours and shapes, imagine climbing into the image and looking about. See what you can see, feel the colours and the sharp edges, slide along the soft curves and pastel shades, clamber through the cubes. Be part of the image: feel yourself surrounded and submerged by it.

Now begin the Meditation Exercise, holding the sense of being inside the image. As you send down your roots, imagine how it would feel to do this in your image. As you bring the energy up through your body, imagine a parallel being doing the same thing in your image. You are here and there; there and here.

As you complete the meditation and begin to float, bring together the two senses of being and, as you do this, seek to be in your inner darkness in peace and contentment. This is not an easy exercise, but it offers great rewards and gives you a real sense of existing in a wider sense than the corporeal. Be there for some time. When you are ready, return to the present. Make the sign to end spiritual work.

With symbols, it is important that you understand their deeper meaning before you begin. For example, if you want to use the Celtic cross, you need to know that it grew out of the Druidic sign for the Wheel of Life: the Celtic cross owes less to Christianity than to its pagan heritage. Linked into this is the ancient Tao symbol of the serpent swallowing its tail, which stands for the eternity of life, the constantly turning seasons of the year and of life as we are reborn into life after life. To use the Celtic cross when you are meditating is to contemplate the eternity of life and the unending cycles of our existence. It may also remind you that we need to learn our lessons in this lifetime, or face the prospect of returning until we have.

Another option is to use either images or symbols that tie in with a particular Celtic saint or god: this will give the meditation great depth as you will relate to the whole man or woman and not just a two-dimensional character.

Working with St Kessog of Luss, I have found that, over the years, I have come to know him better. It was rather like making a new friend. In the beginning something brings you together, and there is a spark of mutual friendliness. At this stage you may know little about your prospective friend, except that you have friends in common or share interests, which gives you something to talk about. While you are doing that, you are slowly getting to know other aspects of their personality: how they express themselves; any prejudices they may have; annoying or endearing habits. It takes time and effort to move from this to a stage of comfortable friendship, where both sides know all there is to know about the other and where you are familiar with each other's ways.

I feel like that with St Kessog. Visiting the place where he had his monastery was a powerful experience: Loch Lomond is very beautiful, and it was easy to imagine him walking where I was walking, seeing what I was seeing and perhaps even feeling the same emotions that I felt. That sense of sharing experiences was part of a deeper learning for me of the man and his life. Now I feel I know him well. Sometimes he walks besides me and his presence is a comfort and an inspiration. I tell him about my life and we find solutions to my problems.

USING MAGIC

In a land where spirits inspire us, faeries work for us and gods and goddesses are there to be worshipped and asked for favours, it is perhaps no surprise that magic also played a role in the daily life of the Celt. Magic is not, as the fantasy writers would have it, Merlin striding over the mountains killing dragons in North

Wales, summoning paths on the cliffs of Tintagel or weaving spells to ensnare mere mortals in his schemes, it is something much more subtle and beneficent.

To create magic is to use the natural forces of nature, the herbs, scents, waters and energies of our world, to weave an environment to make things that you want to happen more likely to occur. The magician is the person who understands how the land works, the winds blow, the rivers flow and the sun shines, and who can encourage the spirits of these elements to work for him or her.

We have covered much of this material already. Now you need to realise what is happening and understand how to combine all the factors to make your experience even more powerful.

If you are having trouble meditating in your house because your neighbour's children are playing in their garden, it wouldn't be a good idea to try to cast a spell to silence them – you wouldn't hear them if you were suddenly struck deaf! Better to think of how to enhance your own meditation by focusing on yourself and your surroundings so that you become less distracted by outside noises.

Although you want something to end, the best time for this kind of spell is when the moon is growing in the sky: you are going to cast a spell to enhance your own abilities to focus on your own meditation.

Take some paper and decide which attributes about yourself you want to enhance. In this case you want to be able to concentrate better on your sacred space, your meditation exercises and your inner world. Next, decide which god, goddess or saint you want to work with. You may already work regularly with a particular god and you might select him. However, it may be that you need extra help so you may want to consider using one of the Celtic saints, who were great evangelisers and brought many people to the spiritual path. St Maelrubha, who founded the great missionary church at Applecross in the Western Scottish Highlands, was one such person. There are no images of him so draw one yourself or find some pictures of Applecross to use as a focal point on your shrine.

Now look at the elements and consider how they can help you. Fire is an energiser so you might want to play it down by using candles with cool placid colours: pale green, light blue. Scent is important, but often overlooked. You need something calming but noticeable; something that will hold your awareness. A combination of lavender and something piquant, maybe black pepper lightly applied, might do the trick. Water represents emotion and blue water is calming and inspiring. Find a small clear glass vase, or a jar, pour in some fresh river or rain water and add some blue food colouring. Finally, you need to be earthed to become more focused, so choose a crystal that will inspire you; either flourite or amethyst may be suitable.

These are the basic requirements. The more you can enhance the four elements to conjure up the right energies the better the spell will work for you. Think about what you are wearing: a cleansing ceremony and natural fabrics would help. Consider adding an appropriate wood: ash or oak, in this case.

Music would create a spiritual ambience. Different types of sound create different emotions to help you weave your spell. Try faster repetitive music, such as that used by the whirling dervishes, when you want to invigorate yourself, and slower more thoughtful music, such as the traditional church hymns from the Western Isles of Scotland, whose eerie sounds are reminiscent of the Middle East, when you want to be open to the spiritual world.

Casting the Spell
Now for your magical ceremony. Set up a shrine to St Maelrubha, or your chosen god or saint, with plants in the background and place your pictures or drawings in front of them. Place a candle at each side of the image. In front of it burn some charcoal and prepare a mixture of essential oils, just a couple of drops of each that you wish to use. Place the jar of water on the shrine. Now put some earth or sand on a saucer, stand your crystal in

it, then add it to the shrine. Some earth from your normal place of meditation, or as close to it as possible, would be appropriate here.

You are now ready to cast your spell. First, make the sign to start your spiritual work. Now light the candles and drop a little of the essential oil mixture on to the burning charcoal. Connect with all the elements that you are using: smell the scents, watch the candles, touch the sand and sip the water. As you do chant, 'Let the spell begin. Let the spell begin.'

You will feel a great sense of connection as you reach out to the elements creating the sacred world. Now turn your attention to the god or saint on your shrine. Study the picture or image and, as you do so, take in every detail: imagine them as a living creature, see them breathing and sitting or standing looking at you.

Now begin the meditation exercise. As you pull up the earth energy and cleanse yourself with the white light, always be aware of the image of the god or saint on your shrine.

When you are floating, feel the connection to the elements and the sacred world you have created. Sense the presence of the saint or god now there with you. They may appear to you, you may find yourself in a place associated with them, or you may simply know that they are listening to you. Now you must tell them about the spell, why you have cast it and why it is important to you. Ask for their help and inspiration. This speech is important and you may wish to practise it before starting the spell.

Eventually the audience will be at an end and you will find yourself returning to your body. Open your eyes, look around you, then thank each of the elements and especially the saint or god on your shrine.

To complete the spell, take a small piece of undyed cotton or linen, dip it into the water, rub some sand on it, pass it through the scents and drop some of the wax from the candle on to it. Seal it in a second piece of material to carry with you for as *long as you want the spell to work. Finally, make the sign to end the spiritual work.*

You will see from this that there is nothing sinister about it. Magic was frowned on by the early Catholic Church because it empowered people to take healing, prosperity, opportunity and knowledge into their own hands instead of having to rely on the all-encompassing Church. Obviously, if at any time you do feel threatened or uncertain while you are casting the spell, stop.

You can also cast a spell for someone else, but it will work better if they know about it and are there. The image of old crones casting spells to turn princes into frogs or send the beautiful princess to sleep for a hundred years are the tales of childhood. It is true that the more dedicated and knowledgeable you are, the more power you can put into your spells and the more effect they will have, but all magicians in all traditions are warned that they must do to others only what they would wish others to do to them. Do not wish others ill for fear of what might reflect back on to you. If you are going for a job interview, for example, cast spells to enhance your own abilities; do not try to cripple the opposition. After all, they may get the sympathy vote!

Most traditions that encourage meditation also use tools such as chanting, music, ceremonies and rituals to enhance the experience. The aim is to make the meditation more powerful and fulfilling. And, of course, the more fulfilling the meditation becomes, the more we see its relevance and accord it increasing importance in our daily life. It is a rewarding and exciting circle that links our material and spiritual worlds, and slowly and sweetly helps us shift the emphasis from the former to the latter.

14

USING DIVINATION TOOLS

Tintagel Castle stands, a mountainous ruin, on the clifftops of North Cornwall. It is hard to imagine it on a sunny day: somehow howling gales, pounding waves and banshees screaming around the turrets are the only images you can conjure up. The castle is famous as the birthplace of King Arthur and its name is known world-wide, but fewer people know that before the castle was built, the site was a holy refuge.

In a sacred place like this, time seems to take on a different meaning. Our ideas of past, present and future – or, if you prefer, then, now and to be – seem almost redundant as we stand ebbing in and out of history, the ground shaking under the great waves that roll in against the cliffs.

Similarly in Iona, that most holy of isles in Western Scotland, they talk of many well-documented cases where people have slipped back in time and seen the abbey as it was when it was complete, or tried to walk the causeway long since washed away. The past, in these holy places, is still with us. And the future? Who can tell? If you look out on to a horizon of sea and mountains, time might slip and who would know? If your vision blurs for a moment and colours seems slightly different, the air more pungent, the sea more demanding, is this the future or the past?

For the Celt, time was a flexible concept. With ancestors to advise them and traditions to uphold, the past was very much part of their everyday lives. All the great Celtic sagas were based in a semi-mythical past. You might even think of the Celt as a prisoner of what had gone before, where innovation and change were, to some extent, hard to achieve.

Living in the now, the Celt might have dreamed of a more

noble and heroic future. For most, life was probably not un-pleasant. In the main they were not arable farmers so most of their food came from cattle, fishing and hunting with a little grain to augment this. There was no feudal society: rather, families lived and worked together. Disagreements flared up into occasional battles, which were to be enjoyed as much as dreaded. Enemies used to report that the Celts' inability to fear death made them formidable opponents.

With their constant quest for heroic achievements and noble memories, it is not surprising that the Celts wanted to know what the future held for them. In a life where there was little opportunity for change or advancement, their one hope was that somehow they might achieve a noble task to bring honour to their family and so be remembered well over the coming centuries.

Time-shifting attracted the Celt. It was accepted that people could see into both the past and the future and thus put what was happening in the present into some kind of context. This, of course, begs the question, is the future set or can I change it by my actions? If I see that I am going to be robbed, is there anything I can do to change it? This is a very important ques-tion. The belief that nothing can change the future may breed complacency and listlessness: it doesn't matter what we do, what will be will be.

Some people say that our future is like a place further down the river and that as the moments flow past us, if we drop a boulder into the river, it will change the flow. So, the future can be changed by actions we take now. Another way of looking at it, from my experience as an oracle reader, is to see the future more as a kite flying in the wind. At any given point in time, its position is set but if I change how I hold the string, the way the kite flies changes too. If the wind alters direction, the kite will veer with it. In other words, I am not the only one responsible for where it flies.

The future that I see is not only dependent on my actions. I might build a new house and see myself living there, but if a great storm washes it away, my future has changed through no action on my part.

WHY WOULD YOU WANT TO KNOW THE FUTURE?

Druids had the gift of the sight and used it to advise kings and commoners alike on actions to take in the now. Cúchulainn, for example, was warned by the Druid Cathbad that a particular day had a special virtue: whosoever took up arms for the first time on that day would not live long but his name would be known throughout Ireland for all time. Of course, Cúchulainn did take up arms and the rest, as they say, is history – or, at least, legend.

To know the future is to be forewarned. At any given point in time there is a multitude of possible actions we can take. Should I move house? Should I accept this job offer? Should I let my mother look after my children for a week? Should I drive to work today? We ask ourselves thousands of questions every day: wouldn't it be great to know, to absolutely know, the correct answers?

Future-reading is rarely like that. Most of the time I find it reinforces my intuitive knowledge of the actions I need to take. Sometimes it can be helpful in that it points out things you knew already but to which you weren't giving enough consideration. I have a lifelong desire to move back to where I was born in Caithness on the north coast of Scotland. Yet when I did a reading, the answer, to my surprise, was less certain. What it told me was so obvious that I had forgotten it. In my headlong desire to return I was prepared to buy almost any house just to be there. The oracle revealed that to me the powers of the land are all-important and to buy the wrong house would be a disastrous mistake. So, in reply to the question, 'Should I move back to Caithness?', the answer was, 'It depends on the house you buy.'

To know the future can help us better understand the present. If many strange things seem to be happening to you and you cannot understand why, a reading may be helpful. For example, many people who have become great New Age teachers and healers, like Louise L. Hay, Eileen Caddy, co-founder of the Findhorn Foundation, and Diana Cooper, have had moments in their lives where there seemed to be no hope: all was despair, and they say they cried out in pain and bewilderment. Often we need to go through these times in our lives to clear the way for a better and happier future.

Future knowledge may help us not only to make sense of what is happening, it may even help us tolerate the present. If we know that the struggle we are involved in will have a positive outcome, we will be able to carry on at least for the moment. For example, you might feel it is worth working extra shifts to allow your son to take extra football coaching if you knew this would lead to him joining a major club. Of course, it is normally less dramatic than that. He might simply gain an interest in keeping fit which helps him avoid heart disease in later life.

When working with the future, you must always be cautious. Think long and hard before you change your life in any way after a reading. The golden rule is that if you are unhappy about making particular change, then don't do it. Hold the awareness in your mind but do nothing about it until it feels right to you.

Seeing the Future

This exercise is essentially a piece of fun with a serious intent. Make the sign for starting spiritual work, then do the Meditation Exercise (see page 33). When you are floating, seek out the spirits that are all around you. Feel them moving past you and hear their faint whispers.

When you are ready, imagine that you are standing at the side of a small river. You have never seen it before, yet it is familiar. It is the river of your life. Look to your left and see where it flows from. See your childhood, where the river dances and burbles over stones and down small waterfalls; see more dramatic periods from your past and slowly, with help from your spirits, see how the river flows to where it is now, at your feet. Now, slowly, look to your right and see how the river flows on. Is it smooth and calm or does it rush into a gorge and roar helplessly forward? Look carefully at what you see. You may find it difficult to determine what is happening and if that is so turn your gaze back to the present, wait a couple of minutes and then try again. Ask your guardian spirits and angels for help to see. Sometimes you can only see a little way into the future and that is fine: perhaps there are too many options for you to see further. Follow the river as far as you can, then turn back to the moment and look again at where you are.

Think about what you have seen. Are there any changes you want to make? It may be that you are happy with what you saw, or contented. However, it may be that your river is not as placid and calm as you would like; perhaps it's too calm and stagnant. Think about this for a moment. When you are ready, feel your fingers and toes, and open your eyes. Thank the spirits for their help, then make the sign to end your spiritual work. Write down all that happened to you in your journal. It may be obvious what changes you need to make for the river to flow as you want it to. In most cases, however, you will need to think more about it.

WHY DIVINATION IS IMPORTANT TO YOU IN YOUR PRACTICES

If I step off a cliff, I know, of course, what my future will be. I don't need anyone to tell me that I'll plummet to my death on the rocks a hundred feet below. Equally if I plough a field and plant barley in it, there is a high probability that barley will grow in it next year.

For the Celt, seeking advice about the future was normal procedure. No sailor would have set sail without consulting the local wise woman, a practice that continued in parts of Scotland well into the nineteenth century, if not later. Divination was a visible way of linking with the spirits and seeking their advice. Our guardian spirits and angels can see the bigger picture and so, perhaps, are better placed to grasp the outcome of a particular action. Or it may be that, to them, time is not linear so they can move forward or backward in time just as we can move to the left or right, forward or backward, up or down. Time may be the fourth dimension.

Angel Cards are a simple form of divination: you ask the angels to help you select a thought for that day to inspire you. In this case you are talking to angels and they guide you. It is a real and meaningful form of communication.

In the main when we consult a reader or try to read our own future, we are seeking assurance that what we are doing, or thinking of doing, is the right thing. One woman in Glasgow who consulted me was in an unhappy relationship but couldn't make the break. She wanted the oracle to tell her to leave her husband: she wanted to pass the responsibility for her decision to another. Of course this was part of the problem with her relationship and, interestingly, the oracle advised her to stay with her husband and work out their problems. If she had left him, she would have carried her unhappiness with her; it would have affected her spiritual development and any future relationships she might have had.

Often it is not clear what our spiritual mission is in this life. We are all born to fulfil certain tasks, to learn certain lessons and to cleanse ourselves of certain needs. As we progress with our lives, we complicate things further with our daily worries and experiences and may get lost in trying to fulfil our mission. Divination can help us see through the undergrowth to the clear path that winds through the forest. It can signpost where our spiritual path is and how it bends and turns through the trees.

BASIC TECHNIQUES

The most basic form of divination is to toss a coin. Heads I go home, tails I go to the pub. The implication here, of course, is that there is some benefit in taking the winning option. Some people see this as too mechanistic: it is difficult for the spirits to change the number of times a coin will spin, so a version of this is to use three coins.

Coin Divination

Sit in your sacred space and take some time to gain inner peace and quiet. When you are ready, take three coins of the same denomination and put them into a small bag. Keep them as your divination coins. Now think of a question that requires a simple yes/no answer. For example, should I go and visit my sister tonight? Shake the coins in the bag, then tumble them out on to a table or flat surface while you think of the question and nothing else.

Heads means yes, tails means no. And you have your answer. How do you feel about it? I often use this when I feel I don't care if the answer is yes or no. However, once I have an answer I sometimes feel disappointment, and then I know that I did care. If this happens to you, think carefully before you accept the answer given to you. Remember, you are under no obligation and you might prefer to go with your intuition.

If one or more of the coins rolls off the table you should consider the answer void. You might want to check that the question you asked was as straightforward as you had thought. For example, if you have two sisters, one who lives locally and one who lives far away, you might have known that you meant the local sister but you can see that the question was ambiguous. Equally if a coin spins for a long time before falling flat, you might take that to indicate an element of doubt. Check the other coins: if two on the table are both heads or both tails, the answer is clear. If there is one of each, the overall answer has to be seen as 'maybe'.

A far more sophisticated version of this is the I Ching, an ancient Chinese system. Traditionally the user threw down fifty yarrow stalks, but now it is commonly performed with three coins. The coins are tossed while a question is kept in mind and, depending on the combination of heads and tails, a line is drawn. This is repeated six times, creating a hexagram that in itself contains two trigrams each of three lines. There are eight possible trigrams and sixty-four possible hexagrams, each of which is described in the *I Ching Book of Changes*. Once you have cast your hexagram, read the description of it and seek an understanding of the text to answer your original question. If it sounds complicated, it is. Philip K. Dick's *The Man in the High Castle* is an interesting novel that shows the I Ching in action.

Most people choose to go to another person and this is called a reading. If you wish to have a reading done for you, ask your friends for a recommendation or approach a member of one of the growing number of professional bodies, such as the British Astrological and Psychic Society.

When you meet the reader, it is important that you feel comfortable with them. As the reading proceeds, remember that you are in charge and can stop it at any time. A good reader has nothing to prove to you, so do not try to confuse them: the more you contribute to the reading, the more you will get out of it. If you don't think they can do what they say they can do, then you should not be with them. If, at the end, you are not happy with the reading or have any questions, discuss your concerns with the reader immediately.

There are different kinds of readings, and the best known is tarot. Tarot cards were invented in the mists of time. By the sixteenth century they were already widely used in central and southern Europe. Indeed, even today in mainland Europe many ordinary decks of playing cards follow the same structure as tarot. As with traditional playing cards there are four suits: wands, cups, swords and pentacles. Each suit has cards numbered from one to ten and a jack, queen and king. Tarot cards also include a fourth picture card below these three: a page. There is also a fifth suit, known as the major arcana: twenty-two images of a life journey. Altogether seventy-eight cards.

Tarot has gained a reputation for being associated with black magic, demons and evil spirits. That is not so. When you have a tarot reading all that happens is that the reader will present you with a deck of cards and you, with help from your spirits, will select a number of them. The skill of the reader is in interpreting the cards. Each card has evolved quite complex meanings and, depending on where it falls and how the other cards surround it, its meaning may change.

However, there is more to a tarot reading than the cards. Indeed, most of the best readers will pay little attention to them: they are only a focal point, a launch pad for the reader's own psychic abilities. How this happens is not clear but a good reader can tune in to aspects of our lives. They will talk about the events that have brought us to where we are today; they will discuss the current position – our concerns, worries and hopes – and will be able to tell us what the future holds if we make no changes. Where the future looks less than rosy, they should also be able to suggest changes that we might want to make. Any suggestions they make are not commands, and you should decide later whether you want to take them up.

I do not give many tarot readings but when I do I have to find the right wavelength. I tend to talk about each card, explaining what they mean and how they relate to each other. While I am doing this, part of me is searching for the path, the contact, and when I find it, goosebumps race up and down my arms, hot and cold sensations shoot up my back and I know, I absolutely know, that I am saying what the enquirer needs to hear. Often it doesn't make sense to me but that is not important: the reading is not for me but for the enquirer.

If you want to buy a tarot set, look for one that is very visual. As a beginner you need a set of cards you can interpret without having constantly to refer to a handbook. Juliet Sharman-Burke and Liz Greene's *Mythic Tarot* is ideal for this: based on a series of Greek myths, each card is a story in itself and, indeed, a work of art.

A Simple Tarot Divination

As a beginner you should always be cautious with card readings, but you will probably grasp the main thrust of any reading almost at once. Especially when you are reading for yourself.

If you have a set of tarot cards, take the cups suit; if you have only playing cards take hearts. They will help you find an answer to a question relating to your relationships and love life. Now, however, we want to ask a very simple question: will I be happy in the near future?

Take a couple of minutes to think about it. Would you say that you are happy now? How about in the past? What are your hopes for the future? Think about this, then begin to shuffle the cards while you think. Now concentrate: will I be happy in the near future?

Shuffle the cards again and, when it feels right to you, lay them down in front of you in one pile. Now fan them out so that all are roughly equally visible. Carefully run your finger over the edge of the cards until you want to stop. Sometimes a card seems to stick to your finger, or you feel a pressure to stop. Either way, pull this card out and place it in front of you on the left. That is the card of the past. Next pick a second card for the present and then a third for the future. Place them to the right of each other so that you have now three cards in front of you: past, present and future. Now turn the cards over.

Starting with the past, look at each card. If you have a tarot set try to make sense of the pictures. If you have ordinary cards try to see if there is a pattern. Are the numbers rising, falling or remaining about the same?

The suit is like a trial or a journey. The lower the number, the closer you are to the beginning; the higher the number the closer you are to completion. The question relates, of course, to the quest for happiness. Imagine you picked the following cards:

5, 8, queen.

*All odd numbers in the suit are signs of moving on and strug-
gle. A five signifies neither the beginning nor the end: it is nearer
to unhappiness than happiness but close enough to happier
numbers for you to see and want that contentment. Hence, five
is a card of struggle, of trying to keep cheerful. An eight, where
you are now, is towards serene contentment. You are aware that
there is more to be done, but, for the moment, you are content
to rest and enjoy the moment. In that period of rest, creativity
or travel for pleasure may be implied. The future card is the queen,
who stands for the wife and mother: running the home; raising
the family and looking after family affairs. In this context it implies
contentment and happiness at home and perhaps a time of lazy
nights in with a loved one or, if you are on your own, a time of
contentment with domestic life. There is also a hint of creativity, which suggests that ideas for painting or writing you are
dabbling with may be a part of your future happiness.*

*Once you have thought over the cards and what they might
mean, write your reading down in your journal, saying what the
cards were and how you interpreted them. It is interesting to
come back later and see how accurate your reading was.*

*Remember, while you should not consider it a frivolous exer-
cise, as a beginner you should not take it too seriously. If anything
comes up that you are uncertain about or worries you, seek a
recommended reader to work with you.*

The form of divination I prefer is the oracle. Oracles
acquired something of a bad name after the Greeks used them
in their plays and other writings. In these cases the answers to
the questions asked were as obtuse and open to interpretation
as could be, gaining the questioner little, except in hindsight
when they would exclaim, 'Now I understand the great wisdom
of the oracle.' Good for the oracle, but not very helpful.

With the oracle you are seeking the answer to a question, and
my job as the reader is to help you understand the answer it
gives you. The question may be anything, but the answer, it must

be stressed, is related to helping you on your spiritual journey. I use the *Celtic Tree Oracle*. The beautiful thing about working with trees is that you can have a personal relationship with any tree. If, for example, your main future card was the pine tree, which stands for long-sight and the need to plan for the future, I would advise you to find a tall pine, sit under it and think about what you want to do. By visiting and working with the tree, you can achieve deeper insights than by looking at a card.

When I do oracle readings, I ask the enquirer what their question is. Not everyone wants to tell me and, of course, they don't need to. But it makes it easier to interpret the answer if I know the context in which the question was selected. The question itself has to be carefully constructed so that it is not ambiguous. For example, 'Should I accept the new job I've been offered?' is not the same as 'Should I get a new job?' The oracle will answer the question set and normally little more. You are guided by your spirits to select the cards, and I am guided to interpret them in the way I do. Essentially we are working in a different plane from the material world around us, and I love that sense of being with the spirits.

Many different Oracle sets are available, ranging from *Faeries Oracle* and *Moon Oracle* to Doreen Virtue's beautiful *Magical Mermaids and Dolphins Oracle Cards* and even *Lord of the Rings Oracle*. Find one based on a theme that is of interest to you because you need some empathy and deeper understanding of the topic to grasp the subtleties of the answers given to your questions.

Finally, a simple visualisation exercise. 'Flying a kite' opens you up to the gentle breezes of time. Enjoy it and the future when it comes.

Flying A Kite

Sit in your sacred space and do the Sitting Simply exercise. Now you are relaxed and thoughtful. Close your eyes and make the sign to start spiritual work. Imagine that you are on the crest of a hill. Around you green hills flow away and you can see trees in the nearby valleys. Where you stand is clear and the soft grass is cool beneath your feet.

There is a strong breeze blowing and you are facing away from it. In your hand you hold a string, which you know is linked to your kite. You are looking at the string.

You are flying your kite. It is a special kite. This kite is your future.

When you are ready, look up and see your kite high in the blue sky. Note its shape and colours. Is it dipping and bobbing in the sky or is it steady and regal?

Is it a strain to hold on to the string, or does it feel comfortable? Watch your kite for a while, and feel yourself being slowly drawn to it, merging with it as it sails in the sky. Now you, too, are flying in the sky. How does it feel? Is it exhilarating and fun?

Now look down. Can you see yourself holding the string and looking up? Is anybody else with you? Do you know who they are?

Float there on the wind for a while, looking around and enjoying the freedom.

Always be aware, however, of the string attaching you to the kite flier. Is there anything you want to do? Do you want to soar high into the sky and let everyone see you, or are you content to hang there enjoying the sense of being? Do you want to rush about from here to there and there to here, or do you want just to float and dream?

When you are ready slowly return to your body in your sacred space. Feel yourself back. Take a moment to reacquaint yourself. Make the sign to stop the spiritual work and open your eyes. Sit for a couple of minutes, then write down all you can remember and try to work out not only what it tells you about the future but also the kind of future you want. Can you still feel the fresh wind in your face, sense the freedom and joy? Try to hold those emotions close to your heart. This is the future being offered. Accept it gratefully. And smile.

Part Three

CHANGING YOUR LIFE

15

FOOD

Throughout this third section we will look at how we can expand our spiritual practices into other aspects of our life. For the Celt this was of crucial importance: just as their places of worship were not isolated from the world by wood and stone, so their daily life was not cut off from their spiritual practices and needs.

Since earliest times food has played an important role in bringing people together. Whether it was hunters tracking game or farmers helping each other at harvest time, the pursuit of food has been a communal activity. This is also true of its consumption. Even today food plays a significant role at all major religious and cultural gatherings.

Today, what and how we eat says a lot about our values and beliefs as well as the way we lead our lives and what we aspire to. In our advanced capitalist society, food has become as much a lifestyle issue as our clothes or haircuts.

Given that food plays such a central role, it is not surprising that there is a considerable history of religious thought on its use, preparation and consumption. In this chapter we will look at how we should see food, in our advancing spiritual awareness, what our attitude to it should be, and how, while we are gathering, preparing and eating it, we can further enhance our spiritual experiences.

THE ART OF EATING SPIRITUALLY

You are what you eat. Of that there can be no doubt, yet it is a link that most people are reluctant to make. People who spend hundreds of pounds on makeup and keep-fit often think nothing of buying the cheapest, least nutritious burger or pizza. We need a fit body to let our spirit reach out and function better in this material world. And so, from a spiritual perspective, we have a duty to keep our bodies in tiptop shape, which includes an awareness of what we feed them.

Historically there has always been a tradition of asceticism among people seeking spiritual enlightenment – gluttony is after all one of the seven deadly sins. It is thought that too much food weighs you down, ties you to the material world and hinders your spiritual awareness. There is truth in this. When you meditate at a sacred site, you take yourself out of your material body: you become more aware of the natural world around you, of the birds singing, the rustle of the wind in the trees, the movement of the tiniest creature in the grass. To do this you need to feel light and free.

One morning I climbed the ancient landscape in the Grass Woods in Grassington, north of Skipton in the Yorkshire Dales. It was early on a beautiful fresh late-summer's day. I was led to a sacred grove where rowan, silver birch, ash and hazel stood round a clearing near the crown of a hill. I was hungry, not having eaten since the previous evening, and my spirit soared, cleansed and free. With no heavy meal to digest, I was barely aware of my body.

The Celtic monks followed a strict lifestyle with near-starvation rations and long, regular fasts. In Gaelic, 'Wednesday' and 'Friday' translate as First Fast Day and Second Fast Day dating to when the monks, and possibly the Druids before them, fasted twice a week. Fasting is an emotive issue with some people, and if you intend to do it regularly you must take medical advice before you start.

In our modern world fasting is, perhaps, not easy. Instead, you could cut out certain foods on these fast days. The purpose of this is to help you appreciate food on the other days. Too often in our world we just consume because we can. How often do you go out to buy one item and come back with a basket full of shopping? Food is the worst temptation. All shops have sweets by the sales counter to entrap you: why not give up sweets on Wednesdays and Fridays? On the other days you will appreciate them more and, hopefully, over time you will wean yourself off them altogether and on to something much better for you, like fruit.

Occasional one-day fasts can fulfil much the same role. A grape diet or fruit-juice fast, where that is all you take in for one day, can be a great detoxifier. It is also useful as closure after a period of excess, like Christmas and New Year, for example.

Fasting, or simple restraint, also plays another important role for you in supporting the mastery of the mind over the body, or, if you prefer, the spiritual over the material. Most cravings for sweets, junk or fatty food are just a matter of habit. How often have cooking smells made you feel hungry when seconds before you had no thought of eating? Resist the temptation, and within a couple of minutes you will have forgotten all about it. This is not need, it is a whim, a frippery, and it is exactly this kind of distraction and ensnarement from which our spiritual work is trying to free us. To deny yourself these luxuries is good for you, both physically and spiritually.

Remember that the purpose of these exercises is not to lose weight, though that may happen, but to enhance your spiritual work. Now work out what you will refrain from eating on Wednesdays and Fridays – to begin with, make it something you can easily do without – like sweets or chips – and write it in your journal so that there can be no reneging. Next decide when to start, from the new moon is a good time, and for how long you want to do this, perhaps a month.

Because the exercise is to help you in the pursuit of spiritual improvement, it is appropriate to seek help from the spirits that are with you. Each Wednesday and Friday start the day with a meditation and seek strong will-power and support for your planned restraint.

It is hard for us to to deny ourselves food we enjoy and which is easily available, so don't despair if you don't always succeed. Be grateful for the times when you do win through and just try harder the next time. Over a few months you will find that it becomes easier. You may want to add more things to your list, and as you cut out food that is bad for you – physically or spiritually – you will begin to feel better, and lighter.

WHAT TO EAT

For the Celt, food was rarely a luxury. Most lived at near-subsistence level, growing and catching almost all that they ate. It is unlikely that there was ever a great choice in what was available to them. For us, in the advanced industrialised countries, it is the opposite: there is glut of food. We are surrounded by places either to buy or consume food and drink. Yet we have never been further from the production of that food.

It is for you to decide what you eat, but be aware of what it is, how it was produced and the consequences of that production. As spiritual beings living in the material world we want to live compassionately, harming as few others as possible, helping or inspiring many more. You should apply that idea to all you do.

Of course, it is almost impossible to live on the earth and not harm other creatures, even if they are only single-celled microbes. Jainist monks try to avoid even this by wearing breathing masks and having servants sweep the path clear in front of them, but for most of us such extreme action is difficult to pursue.

You should not shut your eyes to the reality of food production. For example, if you buy some bacon, do you know how the animals that have been killed for you were raised? Are you aware of the conditions of employment for the workers who slaughtered, dressed and packed the flesh for you? Do not turn away and say you do not want to know. You need to know. Your decision to buy that meat has consequences for the animal and the people who work in the food chain.

If you have raised a pig, killed it and eaten the meat, you are aware of the pain of the process. You need to judge how compassionate such actions are. For most of us, that intimate relationship with animals is not possible. If you are going to eat meat or fish you should ensure that it is organic, free range and, wherever possible, find out where the carcass came from. It would also be respectful to acknowledge the death of the animal that has allowed you to eat it.

Vegetarians and vegans are attacked because they cause pain to plants when they pick, chop, boil and eat them. If you grow your own and tend them until harvest then at least you know they have enjoyed a decent life and are being killed with respect and the hope that some compassion exists in such an act.

The most compassionate form of eating is, of course, to eat what nature designed for the purpose: fruit and perhaps seeds. Fruitarianism is not as difficult a diet to follow as you might imagine, especially if you include grains, but it is time-consuming and there are serious nutritional issues to address.

The purpose of this book is not to lecture you on which form of diet is better than any other. I am vegan, and have been for many years; I aspire to fruitarianism, so probably eat a lot more fruit than the average person. On my fast days, I try to eat only fruit and home-made bread. At the colder times of year I add home-made soup. This level of restraint works for me but you must find a practice with which you feel comfortable and which is practical, given your lifestyle.

Consider, too, how you gather your food. Remember, you are what you eat. What would you prefer to be? Someone full of artificial colours, preservatives and junk food, or someone full of wholesome, natural food that is filled with the goodness of the sun and the other elements? This aim, of course, is difficult to achieve unless you grow it all yourself, but you should try to come as close to it as you can.

If you ask, most supermarkets will produce for you, information on how fruit and vegetables are prepared for market. This is almost guaranteed to put you off supermarket food. Fruit is often injected with colour dyes or sugar solutions; bananas are sprayed with gas to make them yellow; it is almost impossible to get a vegan apple now as they are almost all polished with beeswax, and so the list goes on.

My partner and I rarely shop in large supermarkets. When we do go, I am shocked by the bright lights, artificial atmosphere and the stark colours designed to manipulate the customer into spending as much as possible. The false friendliness of the check-out staff only adds to this.

For the Celt, community was everything. We seek to apply this principle by doing almost all our shopping locally in the nearby town. It is true that you cannot get the same range of goods but, given the size of the place, the range is remarkable. To shop locally is to help local businesses, sustain the local economy and, just as important, it is a pleasant enriching experience: you meet friends and neighbours, you get to know the shopkeepers and you keep in touch with local news.

There is, of course, a separate question of what is good or bad for you, and you should make any changes to your diet with the help of a nutritionist or other suitably qualified medical person. Equally, you must be patient with yourself; plan any change with care or it will not last and you will be discouraged from trying again later.

PREPARING THE FOOD

Given the plight of so many people in the world, having the luxury to choose food and then decide what to eat should be seen as a privilege. Too often in our modern world, food is something we take out of the freezer and put into the microwave. Yet it is a pleasure to prepare food for others and watch them enjoy it. It can be a wonderful act of blessing and generosity.

Food preparation should be seen as a spiritual exercise. The Celts used charms and protective spells as they prepared the family food. They recognised that food had a spiritual and a physical aspect, and that some of the spiritual goodness of the food comes from how it is handled, cooked and served. Food left out for the faeries was never eaten afterwards: the faeries would have taken its spiritual aspect. Although it was still physically present, it was of no use to humans.

Treat your kitchen like a temple. Create a pleasant, peaceful environment. Make it a room that you enjoy being in. If you have space, put in a table and chairs. If you have a galley kitchen with no space for a seat, put up a couple of pictures that you like to look at. The idea is to make a comfortable, welcoming space for yourself.

Choose colours that are peaceful and calm: pastels and yellows. Avoid harsh colours that enliven or create conflict – reds in particular should be avoided. When you are preparing the food, focus on that task. Avoid having a television in the kitchen and think carefully before you include a radio. Perhaps all you need is music or even just silence.

As you prepare your food, think of the people you are cooking for. Imagine their delight in your meal and keep these happy thoughts in mind throughout the process. Be aware of where the food has come from, and as you use each ingredient thank the spirits for providing it.

Set out all the ingredients you are going to use. Rather like a television chef, make a show of your cooking. For example, have attractive mixing bowls and chopping boards; have all the ingredients weighed and ready. Try to think of it like a ritual where every step is planned then carried out.

Before you serve it, bless the food.

Blessing the Food

Make the sign to start spiritual work just before you serve the food. Hold the serving spoon in your right hand and connect it with the food, which is still in the pot. Now imagine the white light of love pouring down through your head and into your

*body. You are now a white glowing being of love. Feel the energy
pour into the food and see it energise the food with love. Now
make the sign for closure of spiritual work and serve the food.*

Eating the Food

Just as so many people cook in an absentminded way so the
majority of people eat while they are doing something more
'interesting' – like watching television. To have food lovingly
prepared and cooked for us is such a privilege that the least we
can do is take time to enjoy and appreciate the offering. To begin
with, you should create a pleasant, peaceful, nurturing environment where you can enjoy eating your meals. There should be
no distractions like television or radio, but some ambient music
may be a pleasant background.

Create a sacred space, if you have enough room. Have a plant
or some flowers at the side of the table with maybe a scented
candle sitting in a saucer of sand in the centre. My partner calls
this the candle of inspiration. A small bowl of water completes
the sacred space. Set the table with attractive crockery and cutlery,
either friendly old mismatched cups and plates or a new designer
dinner service, if that is what you prefer.

When the food is served, use your senses to appreciate it before
you start to eat. Take a second to smell the aromas, look at the
different colours and textures and how together they create an
enjoyable picture; perhaps you can even hear the food sizzle on
the plate. If it is appropriate touch it – bread, perhaps, in which
you can feel the different grains. Finally, taste the food and take
time to explore the different flavours and try to name the spices,
herbs and vegetables in the dish.

Now appreciate the food on a spiritual level. See it on the plate
and imagine it glowing with a white light. Think of the time and
effort that have gone into the cultivation of the crops, the harvest-
ing, the transportation, and the time taken here in your own
home to prepare and present it. Appreciate all this effort just to
put a plate of food in front of you. It is actually very humbling.

As you eat, think about these matters, and feel the love and care flow from the food into yourself. Feel the goodness suffuse your body. In this mood, remember to thank the chef. This is also the time to appreciate being with other members of your household. Talk about the events of the day and catch up with what is happening in each other's lives.

By the end of the meal you should be pleasantly full of food and love. This is true even if you have prepared the food for yourself. It is too easy to think that you don't matter, too easy to cut corners and not bother with a nice table or taking time to prepare interesting wholesome food. Don't give in to this – who better to value you than yourself? In fact, I find that when I cook for myself and I take the time to prepare a special meal, it makes me feel great because I have affirmed to myself that I am indeed worth it!

If other members of your household are reluctant to give up their pew in front of the television, you can lead by example. You have to appreciate that these changes are part of your spiritual journey and not everyone is ready to join you. If you explain it is important to you, they should respond. Failing that, you can always negotiate and suggest they sit with you every other night.

Don't present an ultimatum: the television or me. Avoid that at all costs. The most important thing is to remember that this is something you want to do, it would be nice if they joined you, but if they don't want to, there is nothing you can do about it.

What you cook is more difficult. If you decide you are going to become vegetarian and the rest of the family still want meat, you must decide if you will cook it for them or not. I would not. They should respect your decisions and encourage you, not challenge you.

As you can see, food can be a very emotive issue within a household and if one member changes the routine without sensitivity and compassion for all the others there may be problems. Nowadays people may be defensive about eating dead animals. I am not an 'out'n'proud' vegan; I don't broadcast my eating preferences. But when it does come up, the immediate response is, 'Oh I don't eat much meat now.' It is as if my mere presence makes them feel guilty. Within the household this reaction can be magnified, so be tolerant and gentle. If you are changing to vegetarianism, don't announce it: start eating more vegetables and vegetarian dishes. It doesn't even have to be obvious: switch to veggieburgers and sausages. Here in Scotland vegetarian haggis is popular with everyone because it is less greasy than traditional haggis.

Food is a wonderful, joyous aspect of our lives. Sharing it can be one of our most selfless and rewarding tasks. Taking the time to prepare and present special meals is fun, and a sign of the love we feel for our family and friends, as well as ourselves.

However, food today has become a huge industry and we need to make ourselves aware of how the food we eat is manufactured. As spiritual beings in the material world, we have a duty to eat as compassionately as we can. But food is fun too. We can share it with family and friends; we can serve it at parties; we can even give it as presents at birthdays and major holidays. Smile, and have an apple!

16

THE WORK WE DO

Work, as they say, is a four-letter word. There are precious few people who would do their job if they weren't being paid. It is something we endure, may enjoy from time to time but would rarely choose to do. In other words, we spend more than half of all our waking hours each day doing something we would rather not do – year after year after year.

The ancient Celts would think us mad. There is considerable evidence that they had a much more sceptical view of work. As late as the nineteenth century, English diarists touring the Highlands of Scotland complained about the laziness of the Celt. It would be naïve to suggest that this lackadaisical attitude was not in part due to the lack of paying jobs, the oppression of their culture and traditions, and the desertion of their clan leaders to the English Crown (and money). However, it was also probably, in part, a remembered habit. If you have your house, a couple of cows for milk and meat, and enough crops to survive, why strain yourself?

In the early nineteenth century, before the arrival of the train, Highland life still showed many vestiges of the ancient Celtic heroic society where a man would prefer to argue and debate, tell tales or fight battles rather than undertake tedious back-breaking manual labour.

WHY WORK?

We work to earn money to buy food, shelter and comfort. Today self-sufficiency is almost impossible to achieve. Therefore we enter into a trade-off. We do something we may not want to do and in return we are paid a wage with which we can buy the necessities of life.

Over time our idea of what is a necessity has changed. In the Western world we now take for granted that we will have a house, enough food and suitable clothing, and desire other essentials: foreign holidays, new cars, designer clothes and widescreen televisions, to name but some. Because we want more and more material goods, we have to work longer and longer hours. The advent of computers was supposed to herald a new age of leisure. Experts speculated that we would have to work only three or four days a week, that there would be serious social problems because people would have so much time on their hands. Clearly something went wrong. We are now working more than ever and we still need credit to afford at least some of what we want.

Just as work has ceased to be merely about providing the essentials of life, however you define that, it is no longer something we do solely to earn money. For many people it provides an outlet for their talents. Some, for example, are born administrators or salespeople. There are limited possibilities for using these skills in the domestic environment. Other people enjoy the challenge of problem-solving, or creating products that will change our lives. In these, and many other ways, work offers intellectual stimulation and satisfaction. It can be an escape from the tedium of daily life too. When I worked in the civil service I was amazed at the number of people who openly admitted they were glad to get back to work after a holiday spent at home. This, I suppose, might have been a good sign because work gave them something they couldn't get at home.

In the Celtic monasteries workers were encouraged to develop their skills. It was recognised that the development of artistic abilities was of crucial importance to a person's spiritual well-being. At Whitby, for example, in the time of St Hilda who founded her monastery in AD 657 and ruled it until her death in AD 680, Caedmon joined it as a cowherd. He was discovered to have a skill as a poet and the monks and nuns encouraged him, eventually bringing him into their order. St Caedmon is thought of by many as the earliest English (as opposed to Celtic) poet.

Another role that work plays in the modern world is that it allows you to meet other adults and socialise. After having her first child a friend shocked many people by announcing that she was desperate to get back to work, 'There are,' she explained, 'only a limited amount of conversational opportunities with a two-month-old baby.'

Take a moment now to think about the good things that work provides for you. It is too easy to dismiss it as drudgery or to tell anyone who will listen how much you hate it. If that is true, resign. Think of friends you have made, nights out you have enjoyed. Think of the job you do and what you like about it. If there are aspects of your work that you don't enjoy, try to work out why you don't enjoy them, then see if there is a way round this. For example, I used to work in a café and I found that, for some reason, I didn't enjoy serving tables. I discussed this with my colleague and we agreed that she would do most of the serving and I would work more in the kitchen.

Write down in your journal all the good points about your work. It is all too easy to forget about them. The next time you have a bad day at work come home and read this section. Hopefully it will remind you that it isn't so bad after all.

THE TYPE OF WORK YOU DO

As a person seeking to walk a more spiritual path, there are certain issues you need to address with regard to the type of work you do. It may be that you work for a company that makes armaments or exploits workers in the developing world: consider whether this type of employment is suitable for you now; decide whether or not you want to put your energies into furthering the aims and prosperity of such a company. Perhaps you could use your skills working for a pressure group, or using your contacts to set up a fair-trade option.

Certain jobs brutalise you. For example, imagine working in an abattoir, dealing with the killing and butchering of hundreds of animals. No matter how humanely this is done, there is no way that this kind of work can do anything but make you immune to the plight of the animals. And that, in turn, must colour your view of the world around you. It has to. It's the only way you could survive in a job like that for any length of time.

I once met such a worker, retired by a couple of years, in a creative-writing class. His stories about life in the abattoir horrified the rest of the group. Yet he couldn't see it. What was terrible and shocking for us was normal for him.

It is, of course, for you to examine whether or not your job is a positive or negative influence in your life. Are you happy to go to work? Do you look forward to Monday morning? Do you find your work stimulating and enjoyable? Are you able to leave it behind when you go home at the end of the day?

All aspects of your life should link into, feed and nourish the others. Too many of us compartmentalise ourselves: this is me as husband, as office worker, as father, as spiritual being, as me. In truth, these should all be one and the same person. Can you go to work and talk about your meditations or a book you are reading on rebirthing?

For the Celt, working with nature and being in touch with the spirits of the land was all-important. If you have to curb these desires when you wear smart business clothes and sit in a large artificial office with recycled air and work with people interested in the latest fashion and celebrity gossip, you will feel alienated. You are in the wrong place.

THE SPIRIT OF WORK

As you consider the appropriateness of your job to you, never forget that you are a spiritual being in a material world. The main purpose of you being alive on the Earth now is that you have spiritual lessons to learn so that your soul may progress back towards the Godhead whence it came. To do this, we need to spend time contemplating spiritual matters. We need to find space in our busy lives to walk the hills, work with plants and flowers, discover the teachings of others and to meditate on our life's mission. This all takes time.

But your work need not curb those aspirations. You may argue that the more you work, the less time and energy you have to follow your spiritual practices. But work can feed your spiritual needs: it can introduce you to ideas, people and situations that inspire and motivate you. It can give you a feeling of self-worth and accomplishment when you see a worthwhile project through to completion. And it can give your life a structure and purpose that help you achieve not just work goals but personal and spiritual ones.

The perfect job, then, is one that allows you to live out your spiritual practice and does not contradict your values and beliefs. It also has to be something you are happy to do. You have skills and abilities that need to be fulfilled just as much as your spiritual needs.

First, let's find out what type of job you would really like to have. Then we will look at the environment you would like to work in.

Your Ideal Job

Take a sheet of paper and make three columns. At the top of one, draw a picture of a heart, on the next, a head, and on the third a tick. Then draw horizontal lines across the page. Each line in this table should be a definable period in your life. They might be childhood, late teens, university, first job, time when your children were young. In the first column write down what your dream job was at each point; in the second, record what you thought at the time it would be sensible to want to work at, and in the third what you actually did. Having completed the table, take a thick marker and look for any trends.

When I was a boy I wanted to be a bus conductor and then prime minister; the sensible idea was to be come a school-teacher. In my late teens I had no idea what I wanted to be as the sensible option, but I enjoyed politics and writing.

At university I was involved in politics while I studied for a social-science degree that started off as economics and ended as politics. I was still writing, on and off.

After university I drifted from job to job, still writing, and eventually stumbled into my own New Age business. And, of course, I was still writing.

I yearned consistently to write, although I never saw it as a money-earning option. That, if you like, was where my heart was, and while I tried to be sensible and think of careers and pensions, this was what I felt called to. The displacement of my heart's wishes meant that any job, even my own business, would give me only limited satisfaction. And that is a hard lesson to learn. You must follow your heart.

Your Ideal Work Environment

Take some time to sit in your sacred space and think of your ideal work environment. You might want to do this over several sittings. Seek answers to the following questions, and add any others you can think of to the list.

- Would you like to work from home or at another place?
- Would you want to work full or part time?
- Would you like to be able to walk to work?
- Would there be many other employees?
- Would it be in a new or old building, hi-tech or low-tech?
- Would you like to have meditation sessions or group counselling sessions at your work?

As you work through this list, you will begin to build up a coherent picture of your ideal work environment. With your perfect job, you may now have some idea of what your ideal occupation would be. For example, if your ideal job is working with people, maybe selling things to them, and your work environment is somewhere where you would meet lots of 'alternative' sorts, then you might want to think about working in a New Age or health-food shop. If you're a baker who always wanted to be an architect and you envisage a small friendly office with people into animal welfare, vegetarianism and the environment, you need to think about retraining as an architect who specialises in alternative-build strategies.

As you fill in your picture of your ideal occupation, consider what you want to do and where you would want to do it. The third factor is how much you want to earn. Like it or not, there are few jobs where people are paid high wages to do very little. If your ideal job description includes less stress, less intrusion into your daily life and fewer demands made on you, the chances are that you will have to make do with less money.

HOW MUCH MONEY DO YOU REALLY NEED TO EARN?

A good way of starting to look at what you really need to earn to support a reasonable standard of living is to examine what you currently spend and divide it between essentials and indulgences. Keep a daily tally. Count the money you have when you leave the house in the morning, add any you get during the day and subtract what you spend. You'll be amazed at where your money goes and how much you waste on unintended purchases. For example, each day you may go to the newsagent to buy a paper, and while you are there you buy some sweets. If you spend, say, a pound on sweets each day, that is £365 a year. It's enough to put you off, hopefully.

Once you're in the habit of writing everything down, it's quite easy to keep it up. It may encourage you not to waste money if you have to own up to it later. Gradually day by day, week by week, you will build up a picture of how much money you spend on different items.

If you live with other people, involve them when you work out your expenditure if they spend money on you or your needs. For example, if someone else pays the phone bill or buys some food, add that to your figures.

Eventually you will have reasonably accurate annual estimates of what you spend on essentials and indulgences. To these estimates, add one-off items, like holidays, furniture or a car, and items for which you don't pay cash. Check your credit-card and bank statements and put these figures into your tally too. After you have done all this, divide by twelve and you will have your monthly expenditure total. This is the amount you currently need to earn to lead the material quality of life you are currently leading with no changes.

Now, analysing the figures, decide what changes you would like to make in your lifestyle to save money and allow you to work less. You need to re-examine your expenditure to see how much is really necessary. For example, if you reckon that you spend £200 a month on clothes, ask yourself why. What about non-label brands or second-hand? Check all the items you have classified as indulgences. Don't expect to get rid of them all – we need the occasional treat.

When my partner and I did this exercise we were surprised at how little we needed to earn and how much we could easily save. Consider this excerpt of a table for a couple with no children:

Monthly target expenditure	Current	Target
Entertainment	£200	£100
Car	£350	£100
Holidays	£500	£50
	£1050	£250

These savings can be made by eating out less, keeping the car as it gets older, and changing from two foreign holidays a year to one based in a cottage in the Scottish Highlands. Entertainment costs can be reduced further if you seek to spend more free time out of doors, hill-walking or landscape-drawing, pastimes that don't cost a lot of money. The saving of £800 a month, is almost £10,000 a year. And these savings involve making fairly simple alterations, without moving house or cutting down on food, clothing or utilities.

So, you've worked out the type of work you'd like to do and you've worked out how you can afford it. All you've got to do now is do it! Failure is not an option: at Duke University in the USA, in a forty-four-year study, researchers looked at 788 factors that affected human longevity and found that job satisfaction was the top predictor.

17

OUR RELATIONSHIPS WITH OTHERS

The family is the building block of any society, and so it was for the Celts, but their concept of family was wider than our own. To discover the extent of their family, they counted back nine generations, then forward to all the sons and daughters of each subsequent generation. In other words I would be myself, son of my father, son of my grandfather, son of my great-grandfather, back to son of my great-great-great-great-great-great-great-grandfather, probably a remembered family tree of almost two hundred years. If each man had three sons, who each had three sons, then I would be one of 20,853 who could all be called family. In reality, though, the family would be smaller, war, family schism and illness culling the numbers, but still extensive.

All loyalty belonged to the family. There was no concept of the individual and the individual's needs and desires. You did what the family required, and to do otherwise would probably never have entered your head. Equally, one member of the family was responsible for the actions of all. If my distant cousin stole my neighbour's cows, my neighbour could claim compensation from me. This enhanced the conservatism of the family: everyone had to watch everyone else. And, of course, as if that wasn't enough, the Celts believed that your ancestors were with you in spirit form. So they were watching you too!

Collective responsibility and such a suffocating role for the family, would be difficult for us to contemplate today in the Western world. We are all used to the opposite, of allowing the family limited influence on how we lead our lives. Following a spiritual path means that we need to revisit these areas and ask if our journey is enhanced or curbed by being too closely or too distantly connected with our biological family, and what we can learn about how to relate to the society around us.

THE FAMILY

Of course, we could ask what we mean by the family in the modern context. For the Celts the family was essentially the same thing as 'society'. In their daily life, they would have met few people who weren't of the same family or working for the family, perhaps, as craftspeople or slaves. Nowadays the world, in the West at least, is radically different and the old ideas have to be adapted.

In the past the family would have been the source of most of our information and the views and values of its members would have been similar. The family therefore nurtured and encouraged each other. This commitment to the advancement of the family meant that many options and desires that, today, rack our lives simply didn't exist. There is much unhappiness in our Western societies because we are not as satisfied or fulfilled at work as we think we should be, or because our relationships are not as loving and supportive as we want. For the Celts, these desires or aspirations didn't exist. They did what they did to survive; marriage was for procreation, and you sought company and entertainment elsewhere within the wider family. Such a lifestyle may seem oppressive or hypocritical to us now, but for the Celts it engendered acceptance, contentment and even peace. Now, with so many lifestyle, educational and skill opportunities available, that is no longer true.

Today, at least in the Western world, our biological family is no longer as important to us. Close relatives may be virtual strangers and, in many cases, hold views we do not accept. Now we strive for individual happiness and emotional fulfilment, goals that might for many be difficult to fulfil.

Family can, however, still play a role for us. It introduces us to people we would not normally meet, people of different ages, occupations, even races. Nowadays your cousins tend to have different types of job, levels of income, interests, hobbies, and even live in different parts of the world. That variety is good for us and opens doors to cultures and outlooks that would otherwise remain closed. One of my friends was on holiday with her sister in Australia. There, they met cousins they had not seen for a long time and were welcomed, with typical Australian hospitality, into their homes. This sense of openness made them feel good and they came home to Scotland raving about life 'down-under'.

Of course, families can still be oppressive and restrictive. This is especially true for us as we start out on our spiritual journey. Suspicion and hostility may be directed at someone trying to find their path. If you have 'a good job' and you give it up to work on a croft in Lewis, your parents may not understand that your quest for internal contentment and spiritual fulfilment is more important than earning bucketloads of money but being depressed and alienated from all around you.

Different generations have different values. You need the courage to accept that they do not understand, respect their point of view and recognise that their concern is born of love for you. But it is your life and you need to lead it as you see fit. After all, people training to be Druids left their families behind, probably for similar reasons.

In the hurly-burly of everyday life it is often possible to get out of perspective problems and disagreements with members of your family. This exercise should help you appreciate them and their unique qualities. If you have no immediate family, think of people you grew up with and with whom you are still in touch.

Appreciating Your Family

Make your sign for starting spiritual work, then do the Sitting Simply exercise. When you are ready, take your journal and think of your immediate family: parents, brothers and sisters.

Now call on your ancestors, who work with you, to come forward and help you to appreciate your family, to see their good points and how they made you what you are today: 'Ancestors of mine! Too often I forget all the wonderful gifts my family has given me. Help me remember them and love them even more.'

Sitting quietly, maybe with a photo in front of you, let your mind wander, being guided by your ancestors to remember those special times. This is not an exercise to rush. Do not expect immediate results. Sometimes nothing will happen, but then you will find that you dream of a family member, or someone else will mention them.

When you are ready, take your journal and write down what you remember and the emotions that you associate with each of the family members you have been thinking of. Not all memories will be pleasant, of course. If you can, you need to cast those aside and concentrate on positive ones. When memories are so painful that you can't get round them, write them in your journal but don't dwell on them. Leave that for another day when you will want to concentrate on forgiveness. Today is a celebration.

Thank your ancestors for helping you to remember to love your family. Make the sign to close your spiritual work, and take a few minutes to come back to the moment.

Of course, sometimes the problems come from closer to home with your own partner or children where the ties are more than biological. You and your partner presumably wanted to be together: the attraction was more than physical. In this situation, proceed with care. Discovering your spiritual path is exciting and rewarding, but it can also become a little too much for those around you. They may resent the changes you are making in your life or the amount of time you spend meditating, walking the hills or even reading. You need to make a deliberate effort to include them in what you are doing. For example, if you are going for a walk, take your children with you. Explain that you need some quiet time and that they should play over there while you sit over here. It is only too easy to became so wrapped up in what you are doing that you forget to spend some time with your partner and children.

Your partner should be interested in and support what you are exploring, and you should take time to explain what you are doing, why, and how you feel about it. They may also need reassurance that you want them to be involved. If they are unable or unwilling to give that support, or you feel unable to ask for it explicitly, take some time to consider the strengths and weaknesses of your relationship. It may be that the two of you decide, for example, that you need extensive private time to pursue separate interests. This means that you should ensure that your time together is even more exciting and special.

THE NEW FAMILY

The pursuit of a spiritual path can be lonely and even selfish because you have to learn to put yourself first. After all, so the argument goes, if you cannot know and help yourself, what use are you going to be to others? I have never been convinced by this argument because, surely, a large part of who we are and how we think is moulded by the people we have known.

I like to feel I am part of something. I enjoy meeting people I know in the street; I like the idea of having friends who are friends of other friends; I enjoy exploring ideas and experiences with others who, while they may not share my spiritual outlook, respect my ideas as I respect theirs. It seems to me that as the traditional family has become of less importance, we increasingly have to seek out new families to replace the support networks that the old family supplied. These new families consist of our friends and work colleagues, and those we meet at clubs and societies where we have shared interests, or in church or at other religious activities. This new family is a fluid and constantly changing network that, none the less, supports and nurtures us.

Now, of course, with the Internet and email, these communities can be world-wide. There are websites and email groups for almost every imaginable interest and outlook and you can make friends through them, though of course, every caution should be exercised in revealing any personal information over the web.

To Find New Friends

This simple exercise helps you appreciate the friends you already have, some of whom you might not have realised were important to you. The full moon is a good time to choose to do it.

Prepare a shrine with Cernunnos, Lord of the Forest, King of the Animals. Cernunnos is the god I find closest to my own sense of having a good time. It seems to me that, far from being the Celtic Pan, Cernunnos is more like the mischievous pal.

Make the sign to start your spiritual work, then light the candles – white or red are ideal. Sit quietly for a couple of minutes and then, when you are ready, tell Cernunnos what would be a great time out for you. It might be something spiritual, visiting sacred sites, perhaps, or it might be sitting in a pub listening to traditional music with a group of people you know and like. Tell him of your friends and of the friends you would like to meet.

Now do the Meditation Exercise and once you are filled with the white light of love for the third time, hold that sense within you. You are now a being of the light. Approach the temple of Cernunnos and, as you bow before him, feel him pay you attention. Feel his eyes on you and watch him acknowledge you. He may speak to you, though this is rare. When it is appropriate walk backwards away from him. Once you are at the entrance to the hall turn, and, as the walls around you dissolve, feel yourself once again back in front of your shrine. Now withdraw your roots and make the sign to close down your spiritual work.

You have asked Cernunnos to help you and he has acknowledged that. Now you must leave it up to him. But, remember, he cannot do it without your help. Look out for situations in which you may meet new people, for groups or classes of interest, or for people who unexpectedly mention old friends you haven't seen for a while.

HOW TO GET ON WITH OTHERS AND HAVE THEM GET ON WITH YOU

I have noticed many Indian groups sign letters or greet each other with the word '*namaste*'. This means 'my spirit within honours your spirit within'. I feel this is an honourable way to meet others.

Without any conscious decision on your part, you will find that you gather around you people who share your views or, at least, are supportive of your journey. Seek spiritual help in meeting people you need in your life. A woman told me of a time when she had been at a professional seminar and had felt drawn to another woman across the room. The opportunity to chat hadn't arisen and they exchanged only a couple of words. Months later, she had attended an angel workshop and the same woman was also there. Of course they recognised each other and, at last, made a connection. Now they are great friends and go to events and workshops regularly together. Her friend, the woman told me, confided that she, too, had felt something click between them but had been too shy to follow it up. Her subconscious was clearly picking up messages from her spirits who were presumably aware of the two women's compatibility. I think we have all experienced seeing across a crowded room someone who seems to stand out. Almost inevitably you end up sitting beside each other or standing together in a queue. It is important to recognise this moment and grab the initiative. I was visiting St Ninian's holy well at Holystone in remote western Northumbria. As I arrived at the nearby forest car park, I met a photographer. We started chatting and walked together along the short path to the well. The chances of such a thing happening at such a remote site are small so you cannot help but feel it was meant to be. What the purpose of the meeting was is hard to tell. Maybe he had to hear about Celtic spirituality, maybe I needed to learn about other

sites he had visited. Sometimes the reason for a meeting is obvious. Sometimes it is less clear. However, you have always to grasp
the opportunity.

It can be difficult to make the first move. Many of us don't
want to seem forward or pushy. But our spirits can only do so
much: they can have us standing beside each other but they can't
force us to talk. You need to make that move yourself. It won't
always be the discovery of a lifelong friend, but it will be worthwhile.

Keep in mind that no matter how fired up with enthusiasm
you are for Celtic spirituality, it may be that you need to learn
from others. It is important therefore always to ask yourself what
you have learned from meeting a stranger. If you are open and
interested in what they have to say, you will be surprised by how
an apparently unimportant conversation with an old man on a
bus may spark interesting thoughts, provide information that may
lead to a sacred site or simply give you a story to pass on to
others. Always be open. Dismiss no one, and welcome everyone.

From this openness, friends will evolve. Most of us put up
barriers to keep people at a distance and that is often necessary.
But sometimes you need to follow your instinct. Certainly I find
it difficult to drop my guard and welcome people in. But I have
made some dear friends by taking the initiative. An easy way to
do this is to keep with you some calling cards with your contact
details. If you are nervous about handing out your address just
include your phone number. One of my friends has his name and
email. That way you can say something like, 'It's been great talking, let's keep in touch,' and give them your card. Which, of
course, puts the ball in their court.

DEALING WITH PEOPLE WE DON'T LIKE

It goes without saying that, as spiritual beings, we should be
above such emotions as not liking people. Easy to say, not so
easy to do. Sometimes you take an instant aversion to someone

when you meet them for the first time. I find this happens rarely – but it does happen.

Remember, in these situations, that every time you meet someone an exchange takes place: you give out and receive something. The Celts were imbued with the idea of polite courtesy towards strangers. A story told of St Cuthbert makes this point. One winter's day, when St Cuthbert was in charge of the guesthouse at Melrose, a terrible storm blew up and the monks huddled round the fire in their small hall, safe and warm. Suddenly a beggar appeared at the door, seeking shelter from the storm. The other monks were reluctant to leave their warmth but St Cuthbert leaped to his feet and ushered the man in. He was half frozen so the saint fetched hot water and washed the man's hands and feet, as was the custom in those days. He led the man to a small guestroom and then, realising they had no bread to spare, offered him his own supper. For the rest of the night there was no sign of the beggar and eventually, concerned that something had befallen him, St Cuthbert went to the room. It was empty except for six loaves baked of the finest flour and still warm. The monks fell to their knees to praise the Lord, knowing that their guest that night had been an angel.

This story, told of many gods, saints and faeries, shows us that we must be kind and welcoming to strangers because we can never be sure of who they truly are. The courtesy has come down through the ages so that even today, in most homes, visitors will be offered refreshment almost as soon as they enter. It applies even to people we instantly dislike. Try to work out why you have taken a dislike to them. It may be that they remind you of someone else or have an accent you find annoying. Sometimes it is their manner of speaking, or the way they stand, or even the views they express. Once you have identified the reason for your dislike, it is easier to overcome it, to put that feature of the person to the side and concentrate on the rest.

Everyone has interesting ideas or information to pass on. I always think of dogs: when you meet someone new, you should approach them with your tail wagging, anxious to be liked and to like them in return.

Spell to Thank Your Family and Friends

It's always good to thank your friends. Of course you can do this directly: in a hundred ways you can show that you are aware of them and their lives. Occasionally, however, it is nice to give yourself a hug and remember how lucky you are to have such a great family and circle of friends.

For this spell, set up a shrine to your favourite god or saint. This is the one with whom you work most closely and identify. He or she will be your agent. Now for the four elements: you need energising powers. For air, find an incense that contains spices like cinnamon or ginger. For earth, take sand from your favourite beach, gathered from between the high and low tide marks, so that it is energised by the flow back and forth of the sea. For fire, set up a large candle and trim back the wax so that you have a long wick. You want as large a flame as practical. For water, gather some fresh water, preferably from either a fast-flowing stream, or a waterfall: place it in a shallow dish and add some rose quartz. For nature, choose a fast-growing plant like a fern or, best of all, brambles. Add any other natural items that you associate with positive, loving energy.

When you are ready, light the candle and incense. Make the sign for the start of spiritual work. Now taste the water, touch the sand, smell the incense, feel the heat of the flame, stroke your plant and look at the shrine carefully. Listen to the silence of your spirits gathered expectantly around you. Be aware of all the tools you have collected and feel the connection.

Now send down your roots and start the Meditation Exercise. When you are floating, remember the different tools you have gathered. Now you are at one of your sacred sites. A great fire burns in front of you. The sweetest, spiciest incense wafts past on the gentle breeze. You can hear the sound of a waterfall some- where nearby and when you look down you see that you are standing on a circle of golden sand. Although you cannot see anyone, feel the presence of your god or saint. Thank him or her aloud for coming, and feel a great, powerful energy encompassing you; a pure energy that you recognise as belonging to Them. You are still you, but now an extra energy is helping you.

Feel the white energy of love building inside you surrounded by the golden energy of your patron. Feel it rise within you until it is pressing hard against the crown of your head. When you are ready, let it go and feel it as it soars out into the sky above you and, like a huge fountain, see the white and gold sparkling lights race high into the sky, then pour down all around you. Know that these sparkles will seek out all whom you love and touch them.

Think of all those who are special to you. Imagine what they are doing now and feel them being touched by your love. Feel your huge, powerful energy soaring out, and feel the euphoria inside. You love and are loved. And it feels great!

When you are ready, come back to the now. Take a small piece of cotton and dip it into the water, lay it gently on the sand, wave it through the incense and singe it in the flame. Now wrap it in another piece of cotton and keep it safely. If you feel lonely or down, take it out and remember the euphoria of having wonderful friends and family, and a patron who truly loves you. Remember to thank your saint or god for giving you the energy to make this spell possible.

Now close down and make the sign for ending your spiritual work.

This is a precious exercise that leaves you feeling loved and loving. Keep it for special moments, but remember that you can never put too much love out into the world.

18

OUR HEALTH AND HOW WE CAN IMPROVE IT

We are all made up of three interrelated parts: mind, body and spirit. Our mind is very much our personality: it is our own personal computer with all our memories, teachings and under-standings. Our body, of course, is our material machine, which carries our mind and spirit. Our spirit is the divine flame, that tiny part of the Godhead that we nurture and look after: one day it will take us back to the Godhead.

In this chapter we will look at the importance of our health to our spiritual development. We will then go on to examine the link between mind, body and spirit, and finally show why exer-cise is indeed a spiritual practice.

WHY WE NEED TO BE HEALTHY

In many ways we are the architects of our own health. When you look at the factors that take people to hospital, almost 55 per cent relate to lifestyle choices; hereditary issues account for only 18 per cent. In other words, the decisions we make every day about what to eat, what exercise to take and how to lead our lives fundamentally affect our health.

Being healthy is not, however, linked solely to the body, how it is fed and looked after. Rather, it is a holistic concept that requires body, mind and spirit to be balanced. All three have to be aligned and working well for us to be truly 'healthy'.

This complex relationship is explored extensively by holistic medicine, which treats the whole person to prevent and cure illness and, even more importantly, to promote better health. Conventional medicine concentrates on the body part that is not working properly and ignores everything else – for example, the cause of the ailment.

Medicine in the West in the twentieth century was dominated by the thought that alien bodies, germs, cause disease: if we got rid of germs we would get rid of disease. Medicine became dominated by the prescription of artificially produced drugs, to the extent now that in the USA, fatal adverse drug reactions are the fifth largest killer, after heart disease, cancer, strokes and pulmonary disease. In 1994 around 106,000 people died in the USA from taking 'medicine'.

Holistic medicine rejects this notion and returns to a more natural approach. If you went to a holistic doctor complaining of pains in your leg, he or she would talk about your life, relationships, work and emotions, much of which may seem as though it has little to do with a sore leg. But that pain might have been caused by a badly positioned car seat, which is twisting nerves in your back and sending pain into your leg. No amount of painkillers will solve that. A holistic doctor, discovering that you've got a new car with a new job as a travelling salesperson, would make the connections.

To be healthy, then, is not only to be physically well, it is to have an active happy mind and to be spiritually fit. Only when all three elements are working well and in equilibrium can we truly be said to be healthy.

THE MIND AND THE BODY

As a gregarious loner I have a love-hate relationship with parties. I hate to anticipate them, but generally enjoy them once I'm there. Because normally I don't want to go I can actually make myself ill beforehand so that I have a perfect excuse to stay at home. Generally this takes the form of a splitting headache. But it is created by my mind. Of course I know this now so it has less effect. But it shows the power of the mind over the body. Another more subtle example of this occurs sometimes when I have been walking down the road feeling good. In that state of mind I have felt quite attractive and people notice me as I go by. Then, by chance, I catch sight of myself in a mirror: perhaps it is not a flattering view and makes me seem fat. Suddenly no one pays me any attention. This, I believe, is because when you feel good, you exude positive vibrations to which others respond. When you feel unattractive or frumpy, you exude different vibrations, which are not as appealing to others.

Feeling Good, Looking Fine

This is a good exercise to do before you go out in the morning.

Sit in your sacred space and take a few minutes to become calm and at peace. Now concentrate on your breathing. Be aware of breathing in, breathing out. Breathing in, breathing out. Now imagine that as you breathe in, you are inhaling a pale pink mist. Feel it slowly fill your body. It is gentle and beautiful. Breathe in, breathe out, Breathe in, breathe out.

Now you are full of the pink mist and you feel soft and at one with the world. Breathe the mist out through your mouth, and as you exhale feel all the debris of the last day go with it, leaving you cleansed, peaceful and content. Breathe in pure fresh air, breathe out the soft pink mist.

Now you are cleansed, you feel fresh and at peace with the world. Still with your eyes closed, feel a shower of silver and gold rain falling on you. Feel the gentle caress as its sparkles touch your hair, face and hands, making you feel good. You're happy and you feel like laughing. You could dance! You're all a-sparkle!

The shower has stopped and you're ready to face the day. Open your eyes and smile. You're wonderful and you know it! Go to it!

Always think positive thoughts. Louise L. Hay cured herself of cancer by using positive attitudes and affirmations: when someone asks how you feel, you reply almost automatically,

'Fine.' It's said without thought. Hay recommends we should say, 'Great! Never felt better!' and the strange thing is that when you say that, you do feel great, you have genuinely never felt better. The ability to put a positive spin on anything is either a gift, or a skill well worth learning.

A positive attitude is so important. We all meet people who are life's victims, the 'poor me' people. They seem to bring ill luck and bad health on themselves to the point that being unwell can become an excuse for not getting out and meeting new people, holding down a job, having an exciting romantic relationship, and all the other good things that we all want. If you ever find yourself thinking along these lines rush to do the Feeling Good, Looking Fine exercise (see page 209).

Sometimes you can even use your positive energies to appreciate the melancholic inspiration that seems to lie behind so much Celtic music and poetry. The sadness is not easy to explain but there is something about the land that brings it out. It is a wistfulness, a time-old sigh for what might have been, which seems to percolate through some of our most sacred sites. To visit them or hear these poems is to bathe in the futility of struggle.

But to access that emotion at a sacred site, we need to be clear and calm in our own minds. We cannot go there with bitterness or hatred in our hearts: these strong emotions will block our senses, our access to the spirits. Once I had such an emotional experience at Machrie Moor in Arran. On the flat moorland on the west of the island there is a collection of immense standing stones. The atmosphere there is not sad or melancholy but, as I leaned against one of the stones, I was suddenly awash with a great sadness and tears rolled down my face. While part of me shared that gentle grief, another part looked on in confusion, and while tendrils of that silent mourning stayed with me as an interesting shadow, when I moved off I was as contented as I had been before. The experience was more one of detached academic interest than of emotional turmoil. Indeed, some part of me actually enjoyed it.

Another major factor that can affect the mind's health in modern life is stress. It is a major debilitating illness, not only because of what it can do to your mind but for what it can do to your body and how it can affect your spiritual work. After a sleepless night spent worrying about some work problem, it is almost impossible to clear your mind to allow yourself to meditate. Thoughts and anxieties go round and round. You can do nothing about them, but still they run, taking up more and more space in your mind until you feel like screaming.

Stress is almost always present in some form. When I lead meditations, I tell people to relax their shoulders, where stress often manifests itself. You may not know it, but your neck and shoulder muscles are often locked hard like clenched teeth.

Meditation can ease stress, so try this simple exercise.

Losing Stress Meditation

Sit in your sacred space and do the Sitting Simply exercise. When you are ready, take a few slow, deep breaths and now, starting at the top of your head, feel the stress melting away. Imagine stress as blocks of red wax stuck to your scalp and feel it melting within and running through your body and down into the ground. Now work on your eyes, nose and mouth, down through your skull to your neck and shoulders. Feel the lumps of red there, feel them dissolve and, as they flow away, feel your shoulders soften and relax. This may be quite painful, so you may want to stop for a moment to rub your shoulders and the base of your neck.

Now continue: feel the red leave the top of your spine and the muscles of your arms. Work on down through your stomach and hips, your legs. Slowly but surely feel yourself free of the red lumps of stress.

Now visualise a tumbling, frothy white waterfall. Step into it and feel the sharp, cold energies flowing through you, cleansing and revitalising you. Now step back and take a deep breath. Feel the warmth of the room around you. And smile – you feel great.

Open your eyes and stand up. Make the sign to close spiritual work. Give yourself a shake, like a dog after it's been in water, shake your arms and legs, twist your body and shake your head from side to side. It's impossible to do this without laughing! Do it for just a moment, but now you're tingling and raring to go!

Do this meditation at least once a day, especially when you're under a lot of pressure at home or at work.

THE SPIRIT AND THE BODY

The relationship between the spirit and the body is far more subtle. Your spirit chooses where and when it wants to be born because it has lessons it needs to learn. You can visualise the spirit, or soul, as a tiny flickering flame deep within your body, within your heart.

Many religious traditions talk of the spirit as being trapped in the body, but the Celts don't seem to have seen it in that way. To them, death was neither to be feared nor welcomed, it just was. To die was to complete this part of the spiritual journey, and you were then reborn to enjoy the next step along the way. It *does* seem daft to dread or fear something that you know will happen. Better, surely, to accept and then get on with the all-important task of living life to the full.

The connection between the spirit and the body (without the mind) is important because it is much more of a link between the spiritual and the material without the rational processing of the mind. While the spirit may not make demands as such, it senses none the less when things are well and when they are not.

The spirit can help cure the body of its ills. The medical authorities are now grasping the importance of spirituality in treating patients. In 1999 it was noted that sixty-one of the 125 medical schools in the USA were teaching courses on spirituality and medicine. True, in many cases this was to designed so that doctors could help patients cope better with imminent death, but many doctors now realise the importance of asking patients about their spiritual beliefs and how they can be integrated into medical treatment. One recent study in the USA showed that 30 per cent of patients who were prayed for made a better recovery than had expected.

Studies also show that a majority of people believe that their spiritual faith can help them recover from illness, and also that those with strong spiritual beliefs suffer less pain, are more content and therefore happier than other patients. Meditation, of course, has been linked with helping alleviate symptoms like severe headaches, anxiety and depression.

All of this demonstrates a growing awareness of a connection between spirituality and physical health. Many religious traditions encompass suffering and pain in their understanding, seeing pain as a test of the spirit, or even as a gateway to deeper and more profound understanding, which the spirit may even welcome. In some extreme cases devotees cause themselves pain, like the self-flagellating monks.

Also, cause and effect may run the other way: physical illness may be caused by spiritual dis-ease. This idea, of course, is at the base of much holistic and shamanic healing.

Cleansing Your Spirit
Visit a sacred site that seems appropriate to you for this purpose. It should be one that has a strong calming influence on you. Make the sign to start spiritual work and do the Meditation Exercise.

Now you are floating in the orange and red world. You are safe and secure, calm and at peace. Now, for a fourth time, pull up the earth energies and feel the earth fill your body until there is no white light left and you are grounded in that space. Rest for a moment, then pull down the white light, but this time do it slowly and concentrate on each part of the body as it washes through your entire being over a couple of minutes.

Now you are glowing with the white energy of love. Feel it throughout you. Look at yourself and see if it is the same white colour from top to toe. If there are any blemishes in colour take a closer look, then flush out the white light and replace it. Repeat this until you are satisfied that your body is glowing a pure, even white.

Now feel that white light of love radiating from you into your aura and the space around you. Feel it reaching out, clearing, purifying and cleansing. You are now totally white light. Feel the cleanliness radiating from you.

Now bring up the earth energy once again and this time wash it away quickly as usual. Retract your roots and close down. Make the sign for closing your spiritual work twice, and repeat the mantra 'I am clean and pure and protected,' a few times. Take a couple of minutes to feel yourself back in the now, then open your eyes.

As well as cleansing your spirit you must feed it, which, to a large extent, is what this book has been all about. The more you open yourself up to the spiritual world, the more your spirit will grow. The stronger and healthier your spirit, the more you will become aware of what it needs, and the more that happens the healthier you will become overall.

EXERCISE IS A SPIRITUAL ISSUE

For the Celts, the idea of donning designer leotards and going to a chrome and plastic temple to pound away on exercise machines while watching television or listening to plastic pop music would have been horrific. In a world where day-to-day life would provide the physical exercise needed to maintain a body, a fitness gym would seem pointless. Yet in our modern world we even seek to divorce the needs of our body from that of our mind. I have seen people reading the newspaper or doing a crossword while on an exercise bike and the sense that they were not really there depressed me profoundly.

Like any engine, our body needs to be cared for. We should celebrate that and enjoy the attention we lavish on it. After all, our body is a testament to our own lives. Every scar and blemish, bump and bulge is something we have contributed to and something that has a story to tell.

As you pay more attention to your body, you should recognise that it has its own rhythms. For example, some people are slow starters, others are racers, up and away. Some stay up late, others need an early night. You need to understand your body's rhythms, then let them tell you when best to exercise, study, rest or sleep.

Look for the most natural ways of exercising. Hill-walking is good or gentle cross-country running. Dog-walking gets you out, irrespective of the weather, and helps you appreciate the different facets of the elements and times of the year. Swimming in the sea is good, and while people may scoff at the idea, sea bathing around the coast of the UK and Ireland was common all the year round until well after the first world war. You'd certainly know you were alive after a dip in the North Sea on a cold day in January.

Many people cannot accept the shape they are or that their lifestyle makes them. We all want to be gorgeous, but when we're sitting on a Costa Dorada beach it is depressing to see row after row of manicured bodies, laid out more like mannequins than people. Concern for the perfect flat stomach or shapely legs can be taken to extremes.

Similarly people fight against getting old. Ageing is a natural process, yet we all stare in horror as wrinkles appear. Perhaps it is a reminder of our own mortality, perhaps vanity, but more and more women and men are reaching for hair dyes and corsets or consulting a plastic surgeon.

It is all a question of degree. Of course we want to feel good, look good and be attractive. There is nothing wrong with that – indeed it should be celebrated. But the fixation of our society on youthfulness is hurtful and damaging. After all, even the youngest, most gorgeous model is going to grow into an old woman one day, if she's lucky.

Beauty is more than skin deep, and it is a hard lesson we have to learn. Just as health is dependent on a healthy mind and spirit so, I suspect, beauty is more than just a beautiful body but a mind and spirit we find attractive and joyful too.

If you feel beautiful, lead a life celebrating the loveliness of nature and look after your appearance, you are beautiful. Beauty is not only in the eye of the beholder, it is also in the aura and spirit of the one beheld.

Health, then, is far more than taking vitamin tablets, visiting the gym occasionally and checking your blood pressure. It is about maintaining a healthy attitude, conquering the stresses and strains of everyday life and trying to maintain a positive attitude to all that happens to you. It is about exploring and enjoying the spiritual world around you, listening to your own spirit and recognising that, above all, you are your own creation. You are who you are, and as such you are a celebration of life.

Put all of this together and you have a perfect plan for creating and maintaining good health. Think how good it would feel to be striding across the moors, full of positive, enhancing thoughts and with your soul singing to the sun. Wouldn't that be just the perfect day?

19

HOW WE SPEND MONEY

You are what you spend – or, at least, that is how it seems to many in our modern Western world. What type of clothes we buy, what kind of food, what pubs or restaurants we go to, even whether or not we go to the cinema, theatre, concerts or operas tell others a lot about us: our values, our beliefs and our financial profile.

It may even be that what we buy tells us more about ourselves than we care to know. Think of your last major purchase, a car, maybe, or a piece of furniture. Did you give any thought as to who made it, how much they were paid, whether they worked in a safe environment? How about the company you bought it from? Do you know if they exploit workers in developing nations? Perhaps they even fund terrorist organisations. Do you know? As spiritual beings living in the material world we are seeking to lead as compassionate a life as possible, and to do that we must be conscious of all the consequences of an action.

It seems unlikely that the Celts had any widespread monetary system until after the arrival of Christianity. That is not to say that they didn't buy and sell things, only that their system operated more as an exchange: Irish gold for French wine or Cornish tin for Egyptian linen. Celtic society was simple and money had a minor role. You grew or caught what the family needed and any excess was exchanged for luxuries.

In this chapter we will look at some of the questions you should ask yourself before you spend money. We will consider the options for influencing change that are easily open to us and look at how you can become an ethical consumer.

QUESTIONS TO ASK YOURSELF BEFORE
SPENDING MONEY

The first question is, do you really want to spend the money? This may seem like a daft question but it is worth considering. Of course you need to buy food and other essentials, but do you really have to buy that pair of shoes or another table lamp? Do you urgently require another 1980s compilation CD, and was that car ornament truly necessary?

We waste a huge amount of money on purchases that are either spontaneous or pointless. You can become too po-faced about this: sometimes it's fun to buy a frivolous toy or gift, as much to enjoy the giving, or the buying of it, as for any real desire or need to have it. But we do spend too much on rubbish, which uses up scarce resources or creates waste problems. Plastic, for example, takes over a thousand years to decompose. Think of all the plastic you dispose of in a week, never mind a year.

If you decide you really do need the item, the next question is how much you want to pay. When we look at anything, we should ask what we think is a fair price for it. The temptation is to answer, 'As little as possible'. But is that fair? What is the consequence of doing that?

For the Celts, it was a matter of honour that after every transaction, both sides were satisfied with the deal struck. This, of course, involves a degree of trust: we need to believe you when you say that you would not be happy charging less than a certain amount for something we want to buy. Or if you tell me it took you three weeks to make this bed, how do I know that is true?

I once knew was an artist who found she was selling little because people did not understand the amount of time that went into each of her works. As someone starting out on her career, she had no reputation or name that people recognised and she had already realised that she could not charge a lot. But her pieces took days, sometimes weeks, to construct and therefore cost her a lot in terms of her own time, and the materials she used. To sell the works she had to lower the price, but to do so was to cheapen the skills she had taken years to develop.

As purchasers we should not put an artist in such a position. Whether it is art, furniture, clothes or even health care, we should be aware that what we pay for an item reflects on us. One clear example of this is food. The cheapest food is available in supermarkets. There can be no doubt about this: supermarkets vie with each other to be the cheapest. But what does that say about us, that we value ourselves so little that we will seek out the cheapest food? To achieve these low prices, workers are being exploited, land is being exhausted with chemicals and whole economies are mutated to knock twopence off a tin of beans.

We also need to consider whether we want to buy something individual or mass-produced. Mass-produced goods are cheaper, but the options tend to be limited. The table you buy is an exact replica of the one you see in the showroom – indeed, you would be annoyed if the one delivered to your house was any different. However, if you buy a table made for you by a craftsperson, they could probably show you what the table would sort of look like, but the final item would be unique. This is a table that an artist has worked on: he or she has selected the wood, treated it, shaped it and put it all together. They would be able to tell you of how the flow of the grain meant they had to alter the design a little. It would be a piece of art, not just a table. Wouldn't it be better to avoid the sterile mass-produced anonymous goods and use your money to buy something handmade by someone who has put something of themselves into it?

Consider this: wouldn't it be great to meet an artist, discuss their work and show your appreciation by buying a piece? Think of all the additional resonance that object would carry if you knew that it was a picture of where the artist had grown up, or that had been inspired by a dream they had had while travelling in Skye?

The items I value most are those that have a story attached to them. They are ornaments or pieces of furniture I can point to and tell others something about the people who made them or the friends and family who gave them to me. I enjoy this as it seems to me that I am validating someone else's life by recalling how they made mine better. It is a far happier memory than, say, recounting tales of furniture superstores, of long queues, indifferent staff and poor-quality mass-produced tables made half-way round the world.

Another question you need to ask yourself before you buy something is whether or not you can afford it. Today we have access to more credit than ever before and almost everyone has a credit card whose credit limit goes up as the credit companies try to trap us. Credit-card companies make their money in two ways. First, they charge the retailer a percentage on every sale (for small shops normally around 2 per cent, though it can be as high as 5 per cent). Second, they make money on the interest charges levied against card balances not cleared every month. It is in their interest to inveigle you into having too high a bill to clear. As our credit debt rises, the percentage of our income that goes into servicing that debt goes up with it. This means that to maintain the same standard of living, the amount of money we borrow has to increase. Credit cards are good only if you can clear them every month.

Shops rush to assure you that you *can* afford a new dishwasher: 'This dishwasher can be yours for only £9 a month.' Sounds good but ignores the fact that the APR is 30 per cent and that you'll be paying for it for five years.

There is a spiritual concern here because the more in debt you become, the more of your time and energy will be taken up either worrying about it or having to work extra hours to service it, which detract from the time and energy you should be spending on spiritual matters. Because of the insidious nature of credit-card debt, it should be avoided unless you have a very high income and the credit limit on a card is kept low.

THE VALUE OF MONEY

Even if you can afford your heart's desire, you need to consider the true cost of that item. This is not the monetary cost but, rather, the value to you of the money you are about to spend.

There are three aspects of appreciating the value of money. The first is to establish how many hours you have to work in order to buy any item. To work out your hourly rate, do the following exercise.

Working Out Your Take Home Hourly Rate

1. *Get your last wage slip.*
2. *It should show you your annual pay to date. This shows how much money you have earned since the beginning of April.*
3. *It should also show any tax deductions since the beginning of the tax year. Deduct this from your salary, to discover your take-home pay to date.*
4. *Calculate how many months you have worked in the current tax year.*
5. *Divide your take-home pay to date by the number of months worked. This will give you your average monthly take-home pay.*
6. *Multiply your average monthly take-home pay by twelve and divide by 52 to get your average weekly take-home pay.*
7. *Divide this by the number of hours you normally work in a week, remember to take into account any overtime you regularly do, to get your average hourly take home pay.*

If your hourly rate is £10 and you buy a coat costing £120, you have had to work twelve hours to afford that coat. So, when you ask yourself if you can afford it, you have to consider not just the financial implications but also the effort that went into raising the money to pay for it. The more you do this simple exercise, the more you will come to realise the true value of money to you.

The second aspect of appreciating the value of money is to

learn how much you can do with very little. No matter how poor and badly paid we think we are, there are always a lot of people much worse off. To them we throw money away on a lavish, frivolous lifestyle. For many people, £120 for a coat would seem outrageous.

I have known a couple of people who earned very little. Through being with them, I came to see how relaxed I was about money. If I wanted to go out for a meal, I went. If I wanted to phone up a pal and go to the pub, I did do. If I saw a jumper I liked and wanted to buy it, I could. It wasn't that I was earning a lot of money, it was that I was earning more than they were.

To appreciate the true value of money, try the following exercise.

Appreciating the Value of Money

Write the days of the week on seven separate pieces of paper. Fold them up and put them into a dish. Pull out one. On that day you will try to survive on initially £4, to be reduced each week by 50p until you are down to £2. Exclude from this any essential expenditure, such as travel to work, but this £4 includes tea, coffee, lunch and newspapers. And remember, this is for the whole day, not just working hours.

On the day in question empty your wallet or purse of any credit cards, cheque books, even 'lucky' £2 coins. Take with you only your money for the day and nothing more. You may want to take sandwiches with you for lunch, perhaps even a flask for coffee-breaks.

Rather like your 'fasting' two days a week (see page 178), the aim is not to reduce your expenditure *per se*, but to help you understand how much money you waste each day on inessentials. Hopefully after a few weeks, you will appreciate how lucky you are that you can afford to spend more money each day and not have to think about it.

The third aspect of the value of money is the 'opportunity

cost'. If you spend money on something, you can't save it or spend it on something else. This, of course is a concept with which we are all familiar. If I book a foreign holiday, I can't afford to buy a new car. The opportunity cost of not spending money on a foreign holiday might be working less overtime and having hours to spend doing the things you really want to do: painting, walking, playing with your companion animals.

The value of money will vary from one person to another. Workers earning £30 a hour might be happy to work for a morning to fund a new coat. They might recognise that it is expensive but feel that they are lucky to be able to do it and that it weighs favourably against a meal out with their partner or buying a new print for the house.

However, there is another aspect you should consider when you contemplate the value of money, and that is not what else *you* could do with it but what *someone else* could do with it. As we all know, the £10 that we fritter away on fast food might save someone's life in the developing world. That's why we donate money to charities.

BEING AN ETHICAL CONSUMER

As spiritual beings in the material world we need to be aware not only of the true cost to us of what we buy but the true cost to others. We as consumers, through what we demand, can shape what is offered to us. If we demand, for example, that our cosmetics are not tested on animals, then as more and more of us ask for such products, manufactures will supply them.

Taking such strategic decisions makes us ethical consumers. That is to say, there are some ethical and moral issues that will determine which products we spend our money on. As vegans, my partner and I do not eat any animal products, such as meat, milk or butter, or wear animal products such as leather, wool or silk. When I go shopping I place these concerns at the top of my awareness. Other issues, like price or country of origin, are correspondingly less important. I check ingredients constantly to try to make sure, to the best of my ability, that I am not in any way encouraging suppliers to see animals as economic goods rather than sentient living creatures.

Another person may be concerned primarily about the arms issue and would seek to ensure that they were not buying products, and so boosting the profits, of companies that make weapons.

There are many different issues that you can be concerned with and, to some extent, you must choose those that are particularly important to you. In the modern Western world there are few if any large companies that do not have connections with labour exploitation, animal testing, armaments, exploitation of developing world economies, discrimination in the workplace, or funding of undesirable political parties and regimes. One person said to me that the only way to be totally ethical was either to do it all yourself or buy from small one-person-operated companies owned by people you know. There is a lot of truth in that, but some companies, like the Body Shop and Ben & Jerry score highly in the ethical points game.

At the end of the day it is difficult to gain all the knowledge so you have to rely on others. Magazines like the *Ethical Consumer* can help – if you read them, at least you will know what you're spending your money on and what you're helping to fund.

Another option is to look out for Fair Trade shops, which sell products produced by people working with international groups to ensure that there has been no exploitation. There are several different groups with different criteria, but for most of us, buying products verified by any of them will be better than buying them from a normal high-street shop.

Other organisations, like the Soil Association, the Vegetarian Society and the RSPCA, give their seal of approval to some products.

Appreciating Your Purchasing Power

Think of the last product you bought that cost more than £20. How much do you know about how its ingredients were produced? Do you know where it was made? Who manufactured it?

Try to find out. Perhaps a visit to the shop will be enough. Maybe you can contact their customer-services office by phone or email. They should be able to give you the information. The more reluctant or unable they are to provide you with the details you require, the more you will suspect that they have something to hide.

Find out as much as you can. Once you have the information consider how you feel about supporting this system. Are you proud that you have helped people or ashamed that you have contributed to child labour or even slavery, environmental degradation and economic exploitation? You need to be an informed consumer making changes by the purchasing decisions you make.

A VIRTUOUS CIRCLE

Of course the less you spend on frivolous nothings, the less you will have to work. The less you have to work, the more time you have to do the things you want to do. The more you can spend your time doing what you want to do, the less stressed you are going to be and the less you are going to feel that you need to reward yourself.

The less you spend on 'rewards', the less time you have to work and the more time you have to investigate the consequences of the money you do spend. The more you investigate, the more you can make sure that this money is creating a positive and enhancing experience. It is a virtuous and rewarding circle.

It is a virtuous and rewarding circle that frees you from having to work so much and lets you spend more time doing the things you want to. At the same time it ensures that the money you spend frees other people, like yourself, from exploitation and doing work they don't want to do. Again, it lets them spend more time doing the things they do want to do. Makes you proud!

20

A PERFECT DAY

To walk the path of Celtic spirituality is a wonderful thing to do. There is so much magic, so much joy and happiness around us that it seems impossible that, having made this discovery, we could ever allow ourselves to be detached from it. Yet in our modern world this can happen all too often.

In this final chapter of *Walking the Mist* I want to help you plan your Perfect Day, just to show you how wonderful every day could be. In the final section we will look at the next steps for you to take and show you how to keep Celtic spirituality as a central part of your life.

A PERFECT DAY

First, pick a date. For fulfilment and satisfaction choose a day just past the full moon when it is waning. Time of year matters less, but it might determine whether you plan to spend lots of time out of doors or indoors with candles lit. You also need to decide whether you want to share all or part of it with others or whether you want to be on your own. The date you choose should not be too far ahead, maybe just a couple of weeks to give you time to plan and, almost as important, to anticipate.

The aim of this exercise is to try to show yourself how fabulous and enjoyable every day could be. So, try to pick a typical day. If you have children, choose a school day; if you work, choose a work day; if you have regular tasks to do, incorporate them into your Perfect Day.

To seek guidance on which day to pick, sit in your sacred space and do the Sitting Simply exercise. Once you have done this, sit still and try to think of nothing. Let the date come to you. If your mind is too active or you are too restless, imagine yourself looking at a calendar and choosing a date.

Once you have your date, begin work on what your Perfect Day will be like. Think back over the last few weeks and try to remember the times when you were really contented and happy. Jot them down in your journal. Now think of your spiritual path, of what you have done recently and how you felt afterwards; think of things you have not done, maybe things you have read of in this or another book that seemed to call out to you, or perhaps a meditation or visualisation that someone else told you about. Write it all in your journal. Try to think of the foods you really enjoy, not the chocolate bars or carrot cake, but the foods that make you feel better within. Again write them in your journal. To begin with, it may seem like a hotchpotch of ideas, memories, hopes and shopping lists. Take time to sort it out. And, remember, you only have one day so don't try to do too much.

Because this perfect day is going to be in many ways an ordinary day, it is impossible to give an hour-by-hour guide of how to spend it. There are, however, certain main events for you to consider as you plan it.

Start of the Day
Start it before sunrise if possible. Ideally you should wake around dawn. Try not to use an alarm: to wake with a jolt is not a good way to start the day. Depending on the time of year, however, if the sunrise is particularly early, it may be necessary to do so. The alternative is to stay up all night. It depends on you and how you feel.

If you are going to set an alarm try to get a one that will play music, then have your favourite mellow CD wake you gently. Keep in mind, however, that most people wake at a regular time. Maybe you should practise for a few mornings. Normally I find that if I set the alarm for three mornings, I don't need to bother after that.

Once you are up, on this Perfect Day, sit in your sacred space for a few minutes, perhaps with a cup of herbal tea. Take some time to come round and think about what the day holds for you. Then have a shower or bath and ritually cleanse yourself. Use natural products, preferably those that contain no animal ingredients, that haven't been tested on animals and have been made by hand. Wear only natural-fibre clothes and avoid perfumes. On this day, you want to be as pure and open as possible.

Sunrise Ritual

I am lucky in that my shrine is on a window-ledge facing almost due east so I see the sun in the morning as it rises. You may prefer to stand in the garden or even out in a park or hillside to welcome it.

As the sun appears over the horizon, thank it for rising on such a special day for you and feel its warmth and radiance bathe you in well-being. You could even toast it with fresh orange juice and, as you drink the golden orange drink, imagine that you are drinking down the energy and happiness of the sun.

Breakfast

Prepare a special breakfast. Make sure you have time to do it slowly and with care, avoiding radio, music or TV. Perhaps you could make fresh fruit salad or just some porridge. As you are doing this, hold pleasant thoughts in your mind, smile and be aware of all that is going on around you.

If your house is busy at breakfast time, you might want to breakfast early and alone. Even better, you might escape and leave someone else in charge. Go to a quiet place and meditate. Seek calm and strength for the day.

Work

Work should be part of your perfect day as you spend so many days working. Try to travel there in the most pleasant way you can. You may have to use your car on traffic-logged roads but better to use public transport where you can retreat into a private reverie or read an inspiring novel or magazine.

At work try to create a sacred space and spend a few minutes enjoying the peace. Let your mind move over to think about work, anticipate what you are going to do and acknowledge that it is unlikely that you will achieve all you want to.

While work is necessary to raise money to pay the bills, it may well be that on your perfect day, you won't want to work all day. Don't forget when you finish to undertake your end-of-the-day rituals. In my case they involve clearing my desk and putting my guardian, a sparkling pink elephant, on my in-tray. Then I take a moment to acknowledge to myself that work is over and seek to change my mindset to thinking about personal things rather than work issues.

Spiritual Tasks

In a perfect day many of our spiritual exercises would be integrated into our daily life. However, on this most perfect of days, you may wish to undertake special spiritual tasks: to visit a particular sacred site and spend as long as you want there; to meditate in the house during the day when no one is around and all is quiet; to read a book or draw some pictures for your journal.

I would go for a walk in the hills nearby. Normally I don't plan a route, I just set off and am away for as long as it takes. If the weather is particularly bad you may prefer to adopt an alternative indoor plan, although it can be truly exhilarating out of doors in stormy weather, with the primeval elements swirling around you. On such a day you will really feel the magic of life and the sense of the gods being alive and walking the hills with you.

Whatever tasks you choose, always be aware of the world around you. On this perfect day you should be particularly watchful for signs to show where you should go or what you should do. Sometimes it is obvious: a book falls off a shelf; a friend mentions a particular site or even a journey. At other times, while out walking, it is just as if a path opens up. While walking through trees you may see a path that, seconds before, was not there. When I was climbing Pendle Hill in Lancashire, famous for its seventeenth-century witches, I was curious to see what energies I would discover on the crown of this great slumbering mound. Over seventeen hundred feet high, it is quite a climb and the idea of wizened old witches walking up it in the dark seemed ludicrous.

When I was on the moorland that covers the spine of this hill, I could sense the difference in the feel of the land that, to the valley dwellers, might well have seemed magical. There was an echo of the wild magic of the untamed moors of Sutherland. And as I stood there and wondered where, in all this bleak, undulating heather, anyone would have carried out a ritual, a path opened up to me. I left the well-trodden route of the tourists and followed it to a raised hummock. There, amid the heather, I stood and felt a cold prickle of magic. Nothing sinister, just a sense that people had indeed been there.

The Romans might have carried out their sacrifices at the top of Pendle Hill, witches might have danced with their covens, and may still, but for me Pendle Hill was a peaceful, empty place. The only strange thing about it was that when I returned to Pendle village, I had not been gone nearly as long as I had thought. It was as if time had stopped for a couple of hours while I had walked the wide-open spaces on Pendle Hill.

Food

Try to plan your meals in advance and either buy the food or make it part of your Perfect Day to go to a local farm shop or greengrocer to buy what you need. Shopping can be highly enjoyable when you meet people you know or just chat with the shopkeepers. Make food that you want to eat. Try to focus on light, fresh dishes.

Meditation for the Sun Going Down

As the sun sinks in the west, take some time to watch it. If you can, find a space where you can see it sink over the horizon and, as it slowly glides out of view, make the sign for starting spiritual work. Now do the Meditation Exercise (see page 33), and as you float, see the setting sun in your mind's eye. Feel its perpetual motion as it circles the Earth day after day. Know that as it dies and is reborn so are we all. Try to feel that perpetual motion within yourself; accept this knowledge and know it to be true. And as you accept it, feel the calm and sense of peace that this brings.

Think about all that you have done on your Perfect Day, what you have experienced and learned, and then acknowledge that every day could be like this or even better. Know that you are the master of your own fate and today you have learned an important lesson on how things could be.

Now as dusk falls, feel the barriers between this world and the others fall away. Feel within yourself the reaching out of your mind and sense the gliding past of spirits. Send out your calmness and serenity to enrich all the land around you. Imagine a great cloak flowing from you over the land. Listen to the noises of the night and feel them all around you. As the light slowly darkens feel the change in the air. Know that this is the time of adventure and knowledge, of exploration and discovery, of faeries and magic.

Now open your eyes. Slowly start walking home, but take time to explore the bushes and trees around you. You are still open to spiritual influences so try to see the world as they see it: look for the auras of the plants around you and even of the land itself; feel the ebb and flow of the magic energy, and if you are drawn anywhere, go with that flow. When you are ready, make the sign to end your spiritual work and make sure you do this before you encounter any houses or other people.

End of Day

Give yourself enough time to enjoy getting ready for bed. Take some time to write up your journal, adding any pictures you have drawn or poems you have written during the day. Sit in your sacred space and think over the day. Remember not just the good times but also the emotions and ideas you enjoyed. Perhaps you had some spiritual insights and you may want to take a little time to try to understand them. You will probably have had some revelations about your own life and how you lead it – again, write it all in your journal and try to make sense of it. You may need to return to these ideas several times.

Also, do the things you enjoy. If you like a bath at night, make sure you have a luxurious soak with candles and bubbles. If you like to read in bed, give yourself an extra quarter of an hour to enjoy it. Whatever your treat, allow it at the end of your Perfect Day.

Just before you go to sleep, smile and remember to thank the elements for inspiring you. Thank your gods and spirits for their help and, most of all, congratulate yourself for allowing yourself to have such a perfect day.

The Perfect Day Memento
Having planned and enjoyed a Perfect Day, who not plan another? To inspire you and to remind you of your Perfect Day take a small piece of rose quartz, sit in your Sacred Space and do the Sitting Simply exercise. Now take your rose quartz and hold it carefully in, or near to, the candle flame. Remember the sunrise and the sunset, how fabulous they were and how you felt. Now hold the rose quartz in the incense smoke and remember how you were inspired by the day. Place it in the sand and think of the places you visited, even if you only sat in your back garden. Finally place the rose quartz in the water and think of the emotions of the day; how you felt, how happy and contented you were, and how what you were doing seemed so right. When you are ready, make the sign to end spiritual work and open your eyes.

Carry this crystal with you. Let it remind you of the Perfect Day and make a silent pledge to yourself to have another Perfect Day perhaps before the next but one new moon, or certainly before the next fire festival.

THE NEXT STEPS

You have taken the first important steps along your spiritual path. Do not falter now. Connect with the rhythms of the year and use each fire festival as a chance to take stock, see how you are faring and restate your ambitions.

I know only too well how difficult it is to keep these practices going. Pressures at work or from family can become all-encompassing and suddenly another week, another month, another season has passed by.

Take some practical steps. Get a calendar that shows the stages of the moon – many do. Mark on it the fire festivals: Samhain, 1 November; Imbolc, 1 February; Beltaine, 1 May; Lammas 1 August. Also mark the phases of the sun: winter solstice, 21 December; spring equinox, 21 March; summer solstice, 21 June and autumn equinox, 21 September. Every six weeks you have an excuse to celebrate!

Take your journal and write what you would like to achieve in your day-to-day life. It might be to meditate each day, or to spend half an hour in your sacred space. You might want to discover and explore sacred sites once a month. Write down your goals and determine to move towards them.

Think of the seasons as they pass and change your altars and sacred space to reflect the colours and feelings of each season: whites and blues for winter, greens and yellows for spring, bright reds, golds and oranges for summer, browns and russet reds for autumn.

Making the Commitment

On the first of each month take time to think on what you have achieved spiritually over the last month, and plan what you want to do in the coming month. Be realistic and, if anything, aim for less than you think you can do and succeed spectacularly, rather than set ambitions that are too high and only depress you when you fail miserably: for example, you could never have visited a sacred site every day.

Now pick a crystal that symbolises your ambition for the month ahead. You don't need to know anything about crystals, you can do it intuitively. You might choose quartz for giving you the energy to visit sacred sites; rose quartz to help you realise how much you love and appreciate your partner, or tiger's eye to help you work more with your intuitive mind.

Once you have chosen your crystal, place it prominently in your sacred space or on your altar. It will be a constant reminder to you of your ambition for the month. When you sit in your sacred space, hold it in your hand. You could even put it in your pocket when you are out to remind you.

Once you find that this is working for you, switch to the moon cycles. You will probably find it easier to work from full moon to full moon: it is far more obvious in the sky, an almost unmissable sign to you that another month has gone by.

FINALLY

I once heard an old toast that I often use now: 'May your best day be your worst!' That, dear reader, is what I wish for you. Together we have travelled a long and exciting path. We have explored how nature can make your life special, how the beliefs of the ancient Celts can still show us the truly important aspects of our life and how to put the modern world into perspective.

To live like a Celt is to lead a simpler, less demanding life. It is a life that takes time to see and feel the changing seasons, to hear the call of the hills and rivers, and has the time and energy to respond to them. It is a life that celebrates our gods and goddesses and acknowledges the ongoing presence of our saints, who walked these paths before us.

We seek compassion and tolerance in our actions and search for the spiritual truths that are important to us. 'Walking the Mist' takes us out of ourselves, exercises other senses and teaches us to listen to our intuition and follow our dreams.

There is still so much to show and share with you: dreams, herbs, faeries, healing and using your creativity, to name just some. But we have come so far already and it is time to take a seat and admire the view, to look back at our winding path and all around us at the sweeping slopes of the hills, the blue of the sky and the slowly sinking sun.

It is time to appreciate what we have achieved, to see how far we have come and how already the scenery has changed to a beautiful open vista where the spirits roam and our hearts swell in sheer happiness. Here you can feel the magic, sense the inspiration and truly appreciate life. Here, you know you are alive! Enjoy!

FURTHER READING

As my spiritual journey has been unfolding, new and different books have entered my life to reassure, challenge and inspire me. Here are some that I found particularly helpful. For anyone interested in finding out more about the subjects covered in this book, I hope this will be of some interest.

General
David Cousins, *Handbook for Light Workers* (Barton House, Totnes, Devon, 1993)

Sacred Sites
Janet and Colin Bord, *Sacred Waters: holy wells and water lore in Britain and Ireland* (Paladin, London 1986)

Celtic Spirituality (General)
Alexander Carmichael, *Carmina Gadelica*, five volumes (Oliver and Boyd, Edingburgh, 1928)
Padraigín Clancy (ed.), *Celtic Threads: exploring the wisdom of our heritage* (Veritas, Dublin, 1999)

Celtic Spirituality (Christian)
Diana Leatham; *They Built On Rock: stories of the Celtic Saints* (Holder & Stoughton, London 1948)
Noel Dermot O'Donoghue, *The Mountain Behind the Mountain, aspects of the Celtic tradition* (T. & T. Clark, Edinburgh, 1993)
Alfred P. Smyth, *Warlords and Holy Men: Scotland AD 80–1000* (Edward Arnold, London, 1984)

Celtic Spirituality (Non-Christian)

Steve Blamires, *Celtic Tree Mysteries: practical Druid magic and divination* (Llewellyn Publications, St Paul, Minnesota, 2002)

Dáithí Ó hÓgáin, *The Sacred Isle: belief and religion in pre-Christian Ireland*

www.shee-eire.com

FURTHER LISTENING

Music is so important to us. Like most people I have an eclectic collection, but here is some of the Celtic-inspired music that has been particularly important to me and to the people I have played it for at my talks and workshops.

Anúna, *Invocation*
Karen Casey, *The Winds Begin to Sing*
The Chieftains, *Tears of Stone*
Enya, *Paint the Sky With Stars*
Loreena McKennitt, *Elemental*
Loreena McKennitt, *The Visit*
Mary McLaughlin and William Coulter, *Celtic Requiem*
Áine Minogue, *The Mysts of Time*
Paul Mounsey, *Nahoo3: Notes from the Republic*
Gary Stadler, *Fairy Nightsong*
Various, *Celtic Voices*